Praise for Kathy Kwiatkowski and *Stand in Your Brilliance*

"Full of hope and encouragement. Kathy's book is a helpful guide for understanding how to transcend the conditioning of the human experience. The beauty of *Stand in Your Brilliance* is how it continually reminds the reader of their inherent worth and inspires the reader to live from their spirit and take their light into the world."

—Sonia Choquette,
New York Times bestselling
author of *The Answer Is Simple*

"*Stand in Your Brilliance* offers a beautiful reminder of the truth of who we are as multidimensional spiritual beings and valuable guidance for living a soulful life. This book offers a roadmap to happiness by helping you to fully appreciate and honor the impact of difficult experiences in your life. The wisdom offered for how to reverse the negative impact of traumatic experiences lays the groundwork for realizing a life filled with passion & purpose."

—Dr. Sue Morter,
Founder of Morter Institute for Bioenergetics,
Master of Bioenergetic Medicine, Quantum Field visionary,
and author of *The Energy Codes: The 7-Step System to Awaken
Your Spirit, Heal Your Body, and Live Your Best Life*

"A beautiful reminder that happiness and joy are your birthright, this book offers brilliant wisdom for reclaiming that right. Kathy Kwiatkowski combines her years of knowledge and expertise in the field of mental health with spiritual and metaphysical teachings to guide you in connecting with your innate value, worth, and power."

—Marci Shimoff,
#1 *New York Times* bestselling author,
Happy for No Reason and *Chicken Soup for the Woman's Soul*

"Authors write books for many reasons, though the best ones to read are the ones written by people who want to enlighten the reader. This is one of those books and Kathy Kwiatkowski is one of those people."

—Peter Smith,
author of *Quantum Consciousness:
Journey through Other Realms*

"Kathy Kwiatkowski does an amazing job of sharing her story in a way that reassures the reader that she knows what it means to overcome difficulties. She leads by example for how to positively impact the world and live a life of passion and purpose. The energy of optimism and hope that exudes from her message will help you return to the inspirational mission you are meant to be on in this world. Let Kathy be your guide back to your purpose-filled life."

—Lisa Garr,
host of *The Aware Show* www.theawareshow.com.
#1 Amazon best-selling author, *Becoming Aware*

"Kathy deftly and expertly covers an amazing spectrum of healing modalities that guide the reader to the truth of who they really are: an eternal spirit living a human experience here on Earth. Kathy speaks the truth: that we are all one consciousness, that we are never alone, that we are perfect just as we are, that we are loved, and that we have access to guidance from our spirit and Spirit guides all of the time. That we have chosen of our own free will to come to Earth, and that we are not victims. Rather, she teaches that our purpose here is to increase our level of spiritual awareness and connect to Universal Consciousness, God, and love when in our human state.

"Kathy teaches us methods to discover our constant connection to our spirit and to All That Is. She teaches us how we can hear or feel advice from our guides. She helps the reader understand the value of living in the present moment, and the importance of letting go of the fearful storylines of the mind that would take us out of the present moment into the past or future. Every experience we have in life, whether we judge it as good or bad, offers us the opportunity to grow and learn. Kathy teaches us how we can live a Spirit-guided life filled with love and joy.

"Regardless of where you are on your spiritual journey, there is something within these pages that will speak to you and open your heart. Enjoy!"

—Diane Morrin,
author of *Untying the Karmic Knot*

"All roads lead to 'home' in Kathy Kwiatkowski's inspired book, *Stand in Your Brilliance*. In it, you'll find powerful wisdom combined with practical tools that shine a bright light on the path back to what she calls, the 'big-T Truth' of who we are if we should ever lose our way. Kathy's depth of experience, both personally and professionally, make her a masterful and compassionate guide, showing us how meaningful and joy-filled life can be when we allow ourselves to be led by Spirit."

—Gina Lombardo,
Certified Professional Co-Active Life Coach

"In *Stand in Your Brilliance*, Kathy Kwiatkowski delivers a step-by-step path for living from Spirit and healing from our pasts. Her holistic approach blends science and deep inner spiritual work. Her guidance through multiple healing modalities is clear and earnest while supporting us in trusting our own feelings and intuition, and shining our brightest light in the world."

—Kim Forcina,
Spiritual Guide for Dreamers & Creatives

"This book is a must read for all who intuitively know that each of us is on a spiritual journey but might not really understand what that means and where to start. Kathy is not only a talented traditional therapist but also an extremely well-read, highly trained, and gifted spiritual counselor and mentor. Her ability to nimbly move from one form of therapy to another, based on each client's needs and desires, is rare and powerful.

"As a research scientist, educator, and one of Kathy's close friends, I am continually impressed with her openness to exploring and understanding both the science and spirituality of wellness. I simply cannot recommend this book enough. It is high time we learned to tap into our own spiritual knowledge and embrace our guides and higher Spirit (God) for their collective wisdom and direction. Only then will we live our best lives. This book will help you do just that."

—Michelle (Shelley) McGuire, PhD,
Professor of Nutrition and Director of the Margaret Ritchie School of Family and Consumer Sciences (University of Idaho), member of the National Academy of Medicine, and author, *Nutritional Sciences: From Fundamentals to Foods*

"Amazing book of self-rediscovery! Kathy Kwiatkowski has eloquently woven together a beautiful book to help us with our spiritual, earthly journey. This book is a goldmine of information (options) and helpful how-to exercises that you can immediately apply. It is a high vibrational book that will leave you feeling connected and help you on your journey of remembrance of the truth of who you really are."

—Dr. Alan Nasypany, EdD,
author of numerous scientific articles,
energy healer, and spiritual teacher

Stand in Your Brilliance

Stand in Your Brilliance

A Transformative Guide to
Overcome Life's Challenges and
Remember the Truth of Who You Are

Kathy Kwiatkowski

This book contains the opinions and ideas of its author. It is intended to provide informative material on the subjects addressed in the book. It is sold with the understanding that the author is not engaged in rendering medical, health, or any other kind of personal professional services in the book. The reader should consult his or her medical, health, or other competent professional before adopting any of the suggestions in this book or drawing inferences from it. The author specifically disclaims all responsibility for any liability, loss, injury, or risk, personal or otherwise, incurred as a consequence, directly or indirectly, of the use and application of any of the contents of this book.

Editor: Nina Shoroplova—ninashoroplova.ca
Cover designer: Pagatana Design—pagatana.com
Book interior and e-book designer: Amit Dey—amitdey2528@gmail.com
Cover artwork and interior artwork: Cori Dantini—coridantini.com
Author photo credit: Sara Jo Kimberling Photography
Publishing consultant: Geoff Affleck, AuthorPreneur Publishing Inc.—authorpreneurbooks.com

ISBN: 979-8-9876682-0-7 (paperback)
ISBN: 979-8-9876682-1-4 (eBook)
ISBN: 979-8-9876682-2-1 (audiobook)

Library of Congress Number: 2023901359

OCC019000 BODY, MIND & SPIRIT / Inspiration & Personal Growth
OCC022000 BODY, MIND & SPIRIT / Afterlife & Reincarnation
PSY045030 PSYCHOLOGY / Movements / Transpersonal

With much love I dedicate this book to all of you who are seekers on the path. May you feel supported on your journey to find the joy of returning home to the truth of who you are.

Table of Contents

Foreword
by
Peter Smith

*W*e are in the midst of an incredible evolution of consciousness. The mindsets that have served us previously are being surrendered to allow humanity to embrace frequencies that offer a new vibration. It is time to have the conversations that help us to explore our magnificence and understand those things that may be in the way, disguised and lurking in the shadows.

This book is one of those conversations.

It brings insight, understanding, and ultimately light to that collection of shadows we have come to know as conditioning.

Kathy Kwiatkowski has something to tell you in the pages that follow and you will get the best out of this book if you listen to what it offers in ways that transcend human hearing. If you merge with the author; share the intention behind the book; and live the case studies, the personal reflections, and the exercises offered, you will journey with Kathy in a way that serves you in the most wonderful way.

Kathy is a "former" student of mine and I use that term deliberately. She is a trusted colleague and friend these days, and she and I and others like us are bound together as part of a bigger plan to serve the world.

Let's make no bones about it: if you are reading this book then you are one of the changers here to make this world a better place. We have systems and mindsets in place that are holding humanity back in ways that can't be measured, though the solution is simple. We need to pause, take stock, and choose to see things differently, holistically, and pull the pieces of a new world together, one that embraces the best that humanity has to offer.

Stand in Your Brilliance should be a poster on every street corner. We should have T-shirts printed with those words on them in every color and size. Those same words should be embedded on every bathroom mirror, so that when we see our own reflection, that is the caption under our image.

For now this book will do. Know that this author is right on track with the powerful messages she wants to share with you.

This message is more than just words in three ways.

The first is that she has assembled well-established fields of work and written about them in a way that captures their energy and can easily be understood. The wisdom of others is now in one place, so you don't have to get lost down endless rabbit holes.

The second is that Kathy brings her own concepts to life by sharing real stories from real people who have had the courage to journey within and find their brilliance. This, coupled with her personal reflections of her own journey, brings authenticity and credibility to her message.

The third way this is made real for you, dear reader, is the exercises that have been created for you to experience. Do them deeply, powerfully, and thoughtfully and your soul will be grateful for you taking the time to do so.

In these ways, this book becomes an experience, beyond its thought-provoking or research value. It brings meaning ... from someone who has found their own meaning and who is the only type of person that can do that for you.

We all have a role to play in the evolution of consciousness. Know that you have chosen to be here in these times and it is why you came. You chose to be the person that you are ... and you chose to read this book to experience what it contains specifically and uniquely for you.

This may emerge throughout the book, at a certain point, or at the very end, though this book is in your hands for a reason. Look for that reason, find it, and embrace it as once you do there will be no turning back.

May you enjoy the pages that follow. May they open your heart, challenge your mind, and make your soul dance for joy.

There is a part of your expanded being that knows much of this already and simply seeks to remember.

Kathy will help you do just that.

Peter Smith
Founder, Institute for Quantum Consciousness
President, The Michael Newton Institute (2009-2018)
Author of *Quantum Consciousness: Journey through Other Realms*

"Your Spirit"

Your spirit has been with you since
the very moment of your existence and knows
everything about you;
your spirit knows everything you
have ever done;
your spirit knows everything that
you have ever said;
and your spirit adores you, loves you, cherishes you,
truly appreciates you, and understands you.
Your spirit knows those times when you have
been proud and those times when you have
felt ashamed;
your spirit knows all of the choices that
you have ever made; and loves you.
May this knowing allow you to
Stand in Your Brilliance.

Introduction

I am a traditional licensed mental health counselor and trauma therapist turned intuitive hypnotherapist and quantum consciousness facilitator. Over the past ten years I have transitioned to providing counseling that also incorporates a host of spiritual approaches, which will be discussed in this book. In my work with clients, I blend intuitive guidance with clinical expertise.

This book is about transcending the conditioning of the human journey. This book has been inspired by my counseling work with clients of all ages and their journeys, and by what I have learned from my own spiritual journey. For over thirty years, I have been in a helping role with survivors of childhood and/or developmental trauma, religious trauma, environmental trauma, and situational trauma.

Over the course of those years and through the course of my own healing journey I have also been the client, receiving extensive training in cutting edge trauma recovery therapies; expanding my intuitive abilities by working with world-renowned intuitives; and experiencing a wide range of healing modalities (traditional and non-traditional). I have studied numerous traditional and alternative modalities for healing; I have embraced my own healing and discovered my spiritual calling; I have learned how to facilitate energy healing; and I have learned how to facilitate access to other realms of consciousness.

This training, knowledge, and experience collectively form the foundation for the information that I share with you in this book. I include some personal anecdotes about my healing journey and how finding my way back to my spirit has changed my life both personally and professionally. My sharing is not meant to convince you of my beliefs. Rather, it is my hope that you will be open enough to notice what resonates with you and let that be helpful. I hope that this information and my story will help you to know yourself more fully.

Throughout this book I will use the capitalized terms *Spirit, God, Source, Divine Creator, Divine Love, Universal Consciousness, Unitive Consciousness, Oneness, Self*, and *All That Is* interchangeably to refer to the supreme intelligence from which everything has emerged. Additionally, I will use the lowercased terms *soul, spirit, higher self, and true self* interchangeably to refer to your personal nonphysical aspect that exists in eternity and is uniquely you. Thus, *spirit* is your individual spirit; whereas *Spirit* refers to the more universal *Source, God, Divine.* It is worth noting that some teachers speak of the soul and the spirit as the same. Others refer to the soul as the portion of your spirit that you bring with you into your physical incarnation. In both cases, that aspect of you—that nonphysical aspect of you that is currently incarnating—exists for eternity and is inextricably part of your Self.

I would like to offer a few words about how to use this book. A total of thirteen exercises are dispersed throughout the book. They will appear in text boxes. I encourage you to pause, do the exercise, and journal about your experience with the exercise. This will allow you to gain deeper insights into your understanding of the concepts rather than just a cognitive understanding. An open and curious approach to the exercises will yield the greatest benefits for you.

In the pages that follow, I offer numerous concepts and processes. The intention for doing this is to introduce you to the many resources and strategies available for overcoming difficulties, expanding your spiritual growth, and Standing in Your Brilliance. There are enough practices and information for a lifetime of journeying. Remain playful and explore at your own pace. You may wish to try everything; someone else may focus on one practice or concept. For many, this will change over time and you may be called to explore another part of this book in greater detail at another time. There is no right way to approach the information and exercises, provided that you remain curious and have fun. I would like to suggest that you keep the book handy so that you are more likely to feel the nudge to explore. This book does not have to be read from cover to cover, although it is my recommendation to at least begin that way.

Most importantly, this book is about you finding your way back home, to the joy, security, and comfort of being connected to your spirit, to your magnificence, and to the larger Source of Divine Love. My primary goal is that this book will help you to remember the whole of who you are.

You might be wondering, "What does that mean?"

From my perspective, that means that you know all aspects of yourself: who you are as a human being and a spiritual being, and who you are in truth. There is so much more to you than your human self; and what exists beyond your human self is magical and beautiful. Indeed, *the whole of who you are is your brilliance*. You are a spiritual and energetic entity in human form. If this is new information to you, rest assured that you will learn all about these components of you as you read this book. This book is about you. It is in the full knowing of yourself that you can expand into the human experience you intend to have in your current lifetime.

Historically, I have always been drawn to books that teach me how to do something rather than personal accounts of another person's life. That is likely partly due to my personality (I am the "achiever type") and partly due to my profession (spending much of my time sitting across from people listening to and sharing in their personal journeys). I have aspired to provide you with both a personal account of my journey (how I have come to know the whole of who I am), and some ideas that will help you to have a richer, more complete view of who you are and your purpose for being here.

Since this book explores ideas around purpose and spirituality, I would like to share some information about my own spiritual journey. I share a personal anecdote here as a way of explaining how I have developed my understanding of God, the Divine Creator, over time. I was raised in a strict, traditional, Missouri Synod Lutheran Church. This is the more conservative branch of the Lutheran denomination. As an adult, I transitioned to the Evangelical Lutheran Church of America, a more liberal branch. I grew up hearing the message that I was "a sinner who needed forgiveness." As long as I can remember, I consciously refused to accept that message. That message felt untrue to me, and it made me feel scared and bad, as though I was fatally flawed.

There was another problem with the "sinner" message. In my little kid's mind, being a sinner did not jive with the other messages of "being a child of God" and "God is Love." These days I put myself more in the camp of spiritual versus religious (see chapter 3).

I currently frame being a "sinner" as being human. To be a sinner is to have human desires and impulses—a human personality. To me, it does not make sense to feel bad about being human. Maybe you could ask yourself, "What if sin were simply missing the point of human existence?" This is my current belief system, and I am owning that up front as a point of clarification.

Now I view self-forgiveness as returning to my spirit, connecting to Divine Source, and remembering the truth of who I am; I see forgiveness of others as seeing them as their spirit. In this context, the message that God is Love rings absolutely true. We are all inextricably connected to the field of Divine Love that is God, and the human journey is about finding our way back to Divine Love, back to our wholeness, back to our knowing of the fullness of the Divine Creator that we emerged from and are also a part of.

Until twelve years ago, I was completely unaware that many legitimate mental health professionals and researchers—including psychologists, psychiatrists, and counselors—have studied and written about the realm of the nonphysical. Additionally, there are processes available for accessing the nonphysical realm to directly receive messages and healing for current physical experiences.

It is important to clarify here that there is a distinct difference between mental health conditions that involve delusions and hallucinations versus communication with entities in the nonphysical realm. In fact, many clients I have seen over the years have been relieved to be able to openly talk about their intuitive experiences, when meeting with me, without being viewed as "crazy."

Throughout this book I will present information about the realm of the nonphysical and will share experiences I have personally had in the nonphysical realm. I will also share practices I have found helpful for increasing one's ability to sense and experience the support available from the nonphysical realm.

I wrote this book because I was guided to do so! My guides have shown me the finished product. Similarly, much of what I now do professionally and personally is the result of my guidance.

You might be wondering from where and from whom I get guidance. The answer is that I receive guidance from my own spirit, my guides and God. Guides are our helpers in the nonphysical realm. They are spiritual and energetic entities that assist us here on the Earth plane. Your spirit, the nonphysical aspect of you that exists beyond your physical self, is also a source of support for you and guides you.

Guides can communicate with us in a variety of ways. When I get messages it is typically through hearing them, as if they were speaking to me (clairaudience) or by just intuitively knowing (claircognizance). In this instance, I was given a visual image of what the book would actually look like once completed (clairvoyance). I was confident that I would be guided throughout the process of writing. We have divine support and guidance available to us at all times, but we often do not know when it is happening. I had a knowing that this book would be as much for me and my growth as it would be for those of you who read it.

My heart's desire is that this book is profoundly helpful for you at this time on your journey. Trust that there is a good reason why this book has come into your experience at this time.

Big Love,

Kathy

Chapter 1

Everything Has Meaning

How Your Early Childhood Experiences Shape the Remainder of Your Journey

The Journey Begins

The experience of coming into human form, in and of itself, is difficult. After all, you are bringing your energy, your consciousness, into a human form. This is the process of your spirit incarnating into human existence.

If you experienced birth trauma in the form of having a mother who was anxious, depressed, or angry during pregnancy, or if you were born premature, or had some other kind of birth complication, that adds to the difficulty and the impact on your energy and your psyche.

Scientists now know that the "memories" of these early in utero and birth experiences can be stored in your cells. Indeed, when you experience trauma during critical stages of development, permanent changes can occur in your cells' genetic material. For example, changes have been found in the CD45 cells (cells that evoke an immune response) in the immune system of adult survivors of childhood trauma. A description of the research findings about the CD45 cells can be found in Bessel van der Kolk's landmark book *The Body Keeps the Score: Brain, Mind, and Body in the Healing of Trauma.*

Your very early memories are subconscious memories. They are stored in the subconscious mind and in the field of stored consciousness — a realm of consciousness beyond present consciousness (more on that later). Once you are born, your early environmental experiences greatly shape and influence your view of yourself and of the world. These experiences are key to the formation of your personality. When you come into human form, in the womb, there is an interplay of your spirit, your human brain and nervous system, and your developing personality.

You are a spiritual and energetic being on a human journey. You have an energetic field that runs through you and extends beyond you. This energy field is your spirit. Your spirit is a glorious, big, bright, brilliant, light-filled energy that holds knowledge and intelligence. You are made of everything in the universe.

While your journey is special and unique to you, there are things that all of us, as humans, want to experience on our journeys. As children we want to have joy, ease, and fun. Childhood is when we are still most in touch with our spirit. Children want to be seen, to feel loved and nurtured, to feel special and important, to feel safe and protected, to feel powerful, to feel delighted in and good enough, to feel accepted, and to have a sense of belonging. These are our core attachment and emotional needs. We all have them—all of them—starting from when we are very young. These needs exist from when we are newborn babies coming into the world and from even earlier, while still in the womb.

In the womb we can feel and sense the energies of our mother, whether they be excitement, hopefulness, love, worry, or despair. We feel them all.

When any of these early attachment needs are unmet, the human journey becomes harder. When this happens, we can lose touch with our spirit and our intuitive knowing of our wholeness and magnificence. It is at this moment that human suffering begins, both consciously and unconsciously. In a nutshell, the root of core suffering lies in forgetting the basic fact that you are whole and you are magnificence. Conversely, relief from core suffering comes with reconnecting to the magnificence of your spirit. Once you remember your wholeness and your magnificence, navigating situational suffering is more manageable.

Personal Anecdote: Feeling All Alone

From the stories I heard growing up, I know that the entry of my spirit into a physical form (my body) in my current lifetime was not easy for me. However, I have only come to fully appreciate the depth of how this affected me as I have progressed on my journey back to the wholeness of who I am.

I was born underweight, the second born of twins, the youngest of four children in my family. The story as I know it is that I had to be cared for in the hospital for a few days, while my mother and twin brother went home. I always thought that would have been my first experience of feeling left, of feeling all alone. However, a few years ago, when

I did a Lifespan Integration (LI) session focusing on my birth experience, I re-experienced an in-the-womb feeling of being left behind by my brother, as he was born and I was still in the womb for another twenty minutes. (LI is a supportive trauma recovery therapy that will be discussed later in chapter 11.)

That memory and knowing came as one; it was a full-body visceral feeling of loss that made me gasp. It was as if I could sense myself at the time having the frantic feeling of "Wait! Don't go! Wait for me!"

I have always known the story of what happened: that after my brother was born, "everything stopped"; and it was only because the doctor and nurses were aware that my mother was carrying twins that they knew to get things going again. However, I had never before experienced and felt that deep intense sensation of panic, of being left behind that I felt that day in the Lifespan Integration session. That implicit "felt memory" was released from my body, my cells. Re-experiencing that feeling enabled me to heal the subconscious memory of being left behind.

When we come into physical form, we are bringing some portion of our energy field, our spirit, into a denser form. We are leaving the realm of the nonphysical to come to the classroom of planet Earth to have an embodied experience.

The timing of when we bring our energy, our spirit, into the human fetus varies. Consequently, the amount of time that your spirit spends in the fetus can also vary. I learned through hypnosis, while doing a regression to the womb, that my spirit did not spend much time in the womb. My spirit pretty much dropped into the fetus shortly before birth. Maybe that was because that little fetus was malnourished and hungry (although strong) and my spirit was not meant to experience that hunger for an extended period of time in utero.

Or maybe that was because it was a tight squeeze in there. After all, my twin was full sized and my mother was a slender person. I am not sure, but what I do know is that all experiences in utero and in the first weeks of life can have profound impacts on one's sense of safety in the world. For me, it left me with a nagging feeling of being alone and on my own.

That nagging feeling was reinforced not long after when, at the age of five, I was put in the hospital for what I am told was five days of allergy testing, because of being underweight. My memory of that experience is hours of being alone, on my own in my hospital room. I would be awakened throughout the night with someone coming to take my blood. I remember the nurses sitting with me and my family occasionally visiting. I believe my parents were not allowed to stay with me 24/7 like parents can do now. At least, that is not my felt memory of it. It was confusing and I was lonely.

There is one more aspect to this feeling of being on my own that goes back even further. This experience came to light in the past few years during a session with an intuitive energy medicine practitioner. In that session, the information came through that my soul, from the very beginning, struggled with leaving the realm of eternal consciousness and with losing connection to the support of Source. In essence my spirit was ambivalent about coming back to the Earthly classroom. It was as though my spirit got to the departure point (the metaphoric edge of the diving board) and needed a gentle push.

When we take the leap to come back to Earth, yet again, for another journey, we know the journey will involve going through the process of forgetting our wholeness and having to find our way back to it.

As one of my teachers says, "That is the game."

We leave the spiritual realm to go on a journey "on our own" for a variety of reasons and with a purpose. We are never actually on our own, but we do not know that in the early years of the human journey. As young children we believe that our only supports are the other humans in our world, and our sense of safety depends on that connection. It is all we know.

I was the youngest of four children in a family with a mother who was overwhelmed with the responsibility of caregiving and a father who was overwhelmed with providing. Both were doing their best, but the chaos of that kind of environment is felt energetically by the children who learn quickly to not look for support. I have no recollection of reaching out for support, although I must have from time to time. It is our natural human tendency to reach out for connection and assistance but this natural inclination can also be unlearned.

I have very clear memories of feeling confused and hurt and not going to anyone for comfort. I believe I felt that seeking support would not help and, therefore, I decided to deal with things myself. Even to this day, I continue to discover ways in which I unconsciously go through life from the mindset of *It's up to me, You are not going to help me*, and therefore, choosing to not ask for support from those around me and completely forgetting to turn to my divine supports. Maybe this response is an expected part of the human condition that needs to be overcome. Staying mindful of that tendency and choosing to be open to support is a daily practice for me. Asking for help and support has been one of my major life challenges, and learning to do so has led to some of my most profound spurts of growth.

Everything that we experience has meaning and can be used to advance growth on the spiritual path. Think of it this way: it is like walking into the wind. If you walk forward into a strong wind, even though it may be hard, the resistance enables you to feel your power.

Feeling Alone in Past Lives

So far I have talked about my current incarnation, this current life experience. However, the theme of being on my own has also shown up in my past life regressions (PLRs). I will say more later about the concept of past lives in chapter 3.

Years ago, I attended an I Can Do It! Conference. In case you are not familiar with this event, it is a large conference run by Hay House that draws in a couple of thousand people, featuring intuitives, mediums, and other spiritual teachers who give workshops. I did one of my first past life regressions (PLRs) via the hypnotic suggestions of author and medical doctor Brian Weiss at that event. During this group PLR, I journeyed to an incarnation in which I was a young street kid, getting food from the garbage cans in an alley behind some restaurants. The streets were cobblestone, and the attire people were wearing was straight out of what you would see in the movie *Oliver*. In another PLR session, I saw myself in the 1800s, as part of a wagon train. The wagon that my family and I were traveling in got separated from the others. When the wagon wheel broke and my husband went to get help, I was assaulted while trying to protect my children.

This theme of feeling lonely, being on my own, and believing that it is up to me to solve my problems has appeared in many ways. What I have learned on my healing journey—as a result of doing multiple PLRs, Life Between Lives (LBL) regressions, and energy sessions—is that the theme of feeling on my own is connected to this lifetime, to other lifetimes, and to the experience of leaving the realm of eternal consciousness to come into physical form. Given this, it makes sense that I have a passion for doing whatever I can to help others know that they are never actually alone and that they do not have to do it themselves.

It is no wonder that I so passionately want you to know the truth of who you are. You have a magnificent and brilliant spirit. Your magnificence and brilliance are all of who you are, AND you are always divinely supported.

> **Remember: All of who you are is magnificent and brilliant. Leveraging this everlasting truth on a daily basis is powerful.**

The Importance of Recognizing the Subconscious Mind

False beliefs about yourself interfere with knowing and feeling the wholeness of who you are. To better understand how you develop false beliefs about yourself (which often are outside your awareness), it is important to understand some basic ideas regarding the conscious and subconscious mind.

Much has been written and studied about the difference between the brain and the mind. It is not the purpose of this book to explore those ideas. However, it is helpful to understand that the conscious mind is the part of consciousness that is used for planning, analysis, and logic. It is also the part of consciousness that focuses on keeping us safe. Because of this, our conscious mind references the past, plans for the future, strategizes, critically analyzes situations, forms opinions and ideas, and dreams about desires and wishes. Using the analogy of an iceberg, your conscious mind is similar to the 5 to 10 percent that is visible above the water line. Your subconscious mind is the rest—the 90 to 95 percent below the water line that cannot be seen.

Somewhere around seven to eight years of age, we develop the ability to think more critically. This is when we consciously begin to choose what we believe to be true. Prior to that, we accept as true what we are told, including what we tell ourselves. Around age seven or eight, we stop accepting everything we are told by others as truth and begin having our own ideas.

Consider the huge implications of this, especially with regard to how we experience ourselves, the choices we make, and the trajectory of our journey.

Our experiences very early in life shape our view of ourselves and our world. When those experiences are not positive, loving, affirming experiences, we will struggle with either feelings of unworthiness, unlovableness, aloneness, lack of support, or feeling not good enough. Critical or negative interactions (verbal and nonverbal) occurring in those early years develop into a critical inner dialogue. Many of the negative messages we receive from others and the negative self-blaming thoughts that develop when we have a negative experience ourselves are stored in the subconscious mind, out of our awareness. This is especially true for *overwhelmingly negative* events.

The subconscious mind is what drives behavior. So, you can consciously want to make healthy choices (for example, wanting to care for yourself or wanting to be loving toward others) and subconsciously keep sabotaging these efforts. This subconscious sabotage results in even more self-blame and a critical inner dialogue that disconnects you even further from your spirit.

You may or may not be aware of this inner negative dialogue. Having an awareness of your critical inner dialogue is necessary for healing and growth. Even when you are consciously aware of your inner critical voice, know that there is more of it going on outside your awareness in your subconscious mind. Mindfulness and meditation practices can, over time, improve your awareness of your inner dialogue.

It is extremely important to understand that your spirit does not agree with any of the negative thoughts you have about yourself. These are false beliefs that take you away from your true self.

The journey to wholeness is to know yourself in truth. There are many ways to rediscover the truth about yourself but Life Between Lives hypnotherapy, quantum journeys, and Quantum Consciousness Experiences (QCE) are, I believe, the most direct ways to connect with your wholeness—through the subconscious and the expanding realms of consciousness. These approaches are discussed more in chapters 5, 6, and 7.

The Impact of Human Experiences on Your Awareness of Your True Self

Knowing your true self and feeling supported impact your human experience.

I share an analogy with clients that might be helpful for you. Each of us is special, a unique make and model of car. It can be fun to consider, *If I were a car, what make and model would I be?* Think of your baby self, right after birth, as a brand-new car just off the assembly line. This is when you are most connected to your spirit. Being in close connection with your spirit is often referred to as being "in alignment."

Now your car goes out on the road of life. Sometimes it is a sunny day, the drive is easy, and the car remains shiny and like new. But other days bring rain, mud puddles, snow, sleet, hail, potholes, and rocks. On these days, your car might end up covered in mud, sustain a broken window, or get dented beyond recognition. Similarly, the more negative experiences you have, the harder it can become to recognize your original self. You may even feel as though you (like your theoretical car) have lost your value. The negative experiences you encounter in life may make it hard for you to see the special, unique you that is still there—just like the car might be unrecognizable underneath all the mud and the dirt.

This analogy only goes so far though, because in reality cars can lose their value, but you do not.

When we experience difficulties in life, we place meaning on that. We tell ourselves a story about why it happened. This is the beginning of subconscious negative beliefs about ourselves and the world. These are our personal, deeply rooted stories about ourselves and others. Difficult life experiences can create many types of false beliefs, including *I am alone. I am on my own. I do not matter. I am unlovable. I am not worthy of love. I am not important. I am not good enough. I am powerless. I am weak. I do not belong, and I am a failure.*

These are in complete contrast to the real truth—the big-T Truth.

What is the big-T Truth? Well, it's the opposite of the many false beliefs that can creep into our subconscious dialogues. The big-T Truth is the following: *You are never alone. You are important. You are magnificent. You are lovable and worthy of love. You are enough. You are loved. You matter. You are capable. You are special. You are powerful. You are divine. You are love and light. You are spirit.*

Your spirit knows everything about you, including every choice you have ever made (good and bad). Nonetheless, your spirit never waivers in its love for you. Your spirit appreciates everything about you. The faulty beliefs we develop when we are young lead us to do things to try to be good enough or to feel more powerful. These are parts of you that develop as protectors. Life becomes an endless quest to feel safe, to be accepted, or to feel acceptable. Often this occurs more on a subconscious than conscious level.

Personality develops from this place of not feeling you are enough. It is from this emotional place of not being enough that we develop adaptive strategies, personas that are not completely authentic. This is the false self. These adaptive strategies are absolutely critical to functioning in the world when we are young. These adaptive strategies enable us to find a place in the world and to find some success, but they can work against us later in life.

My early life experiences of feeling alone and on my own led to the adaptive strategy of performing, achieving, and pleasing. Those strategies enabled me to receive the praise, connection, and attention that helped me to feel good enough and lovable. But, my sense of being good enough was conditional and not in line with the big-T Truth of who I am. Overtime, it became exhausting and unfulfilling.

Recognizing the big-T Truth of who we are frees us to let go of the false self and rest into the knowing that we do not have to

DO anything to be good enough, lovable, or worthy. The true self rests in the deep knowing that we ARE safe, supported, cared for, protected, and loved unconditionally.

The Power of Our Inner Dialogue

What we say to ourselves determines how we will feel. Our inner dialogue is intimately connected to our feeling state. We can be our own harshest critics. The bulk of our critical self-talk actually developed from the messages we received early in life, the stories we were told about, and the stories we overheard. At that young age we simply accepted the stories and messages as truth. The messages we receive from the adults in authority roles, as well as peers in grade school and through adolescence, also have had profound impacts on our lives. Over time, we replace the voice of the "other" with our own voice, which in turn becomes our inner voice of self-criticism.

The great news is now you have a choice. You can create a new history for yourself. You can choose to change the critical inner dialogue that has developed over your lifetime, or you can continue to let it tear you down. By changing your inner dialogue, you change your feelings and your experiences of life. If you take the time to really listen to that voice inside, you will hear how harsh it is. You will realize that, likely, the things you are saying to yourself you would never say to someone you love. We can be so hard on ourselves.

Noticing the dialogue is the first step. Once you notice it, you can make the choice to replace it with a kinder, more loving message—one that more perfectly matches the wholeness and magnificence of your spirit.

Try This Exercise: Using the "I Am" Mantra

This is a practice I find very beneficial to do when going to bed.

Begin by taking a long slow breath, bringing all of your awareness to your physical body.

Now, as you lie in bed, having just turned the lights out, take another long breath out to release any tension (you may even want to let out a quiet sigh), and feel the sensation of sinking into the bed. Then, start saying the following things in your mind: *I am supported. I am full. I am loved. I am clear. I am open. I am joy. I am whole. I am life force energy.*

Then, take three deep breaths and start again with more *I am* statements: *I am powerful. I am strong. I am complete. I am love. I am one with Spirit.*

Be slow and intentional with your statements. Think of these affirmations as emanating from your spirit. The *I am* statements you use may be different from mine.

Alternatively, it can also be very powerful to just say the phrase *I am* as your mantra.

Consider taking a moment right now to try this. Wherever you are is fine. Eyes open or closed. Whichever is most comfortable for you. Once you have completed the exercise, take a moment to journal your answers to these questions.

- What did you notice?

- Which of the statements resonated the most for you?

- What was your favorite part of the exercise?

Sometimes when we try to change our inner dialogue, we can have the experience of the voice of the inner critic becoming even louder. In response to our inner affirmations, it may even sound something like "This is stupid. Why are you doing this? You know it does not really work. You don't even believe it."

Or the inner critic may turn up the volume on the old familiar ways in which it puts you down: "You do not deserve this. Who do you think you are?" This is your protective personality digging in, so to speak.

The left hemisphere, the logical, linear part of the brain, often resists opening up to your spirit. Note: meditation and hypnotic experiences have been recorded to activate the right hemisphere of the brain. Your logical, left-brain protective personality can feel threatened by opening up to your spirit. This protective personality is accustomed to being in charge and does not like having to sit in the back seat. What your logical linear protective self does not realize is that opening up to your spirit does not obliterate the logical mind. Opening up to your spirit actually is the process of welcoming the logical mind into the energy field of Divine Love.

As you feel and know and move into your more expanded self that includes your spirit, your protective personality will continue to function as part of you, just not the part of you that is in charge. Your personality is meant to be in service to your spirit—not the other way around. We are meant to live life from our spirit with the logical mind and personality in support of our spirit-guided passions.

Marianne Williamson, a respected spiritual teacher and author, puts it best when she says,

Our deepest fear is not that we are inadequate. Our deepest fear is that we are powerful beyond measure. It is our light not our darkness that most frightens us. We ask ourselves, who am I to be brilliant, gorgeous, talented and fabulous? Actually, who are you not to be? You are a child of God. Your playing small does not serve the world. There's nothing enlightened about shrinking so that other people won't feel insecure around you. We were born to make manifest the glory of God that is within us. It's not just in some of us; it's in everyone. And as we let our own light shine, we unconsciously give other people permission to do the same. As we are liberated from our own fear, our presence automatically liberates others.

To me, this is the definition of opening to your spirit—of moving through the world from the place of your enduring, innate magnificence.

Self-Love, "Big Love," and Energy

Unconditional love is when you love someone "as is": unconditionally, fully accepting them, including their limitations. In other words, if they do something hurtful, you may call them out on it (and hopefully you do), but you do not stop loving them. There is accountability, but your love for them is not contingent on their behavior and attitudes. There is a level of acceptance of the differences between the two of you and you respect those differences.

True self-love is the act of offering unconditional love to ourselves, in the same way that our spirit and Spirit loves us—unconditionally.

**Remember: your spirit knows everything
you have ever done and said. Yet, your spirit
adores you, loves you, cherishes you, and truly
understands you. Your spirit knows those times
when you have been proud and those times when
you have felt ashamed. Your spirit knows all the
choices you have ever made and still loves you.**

You may be wondering, "Why do I need to love myself?"
You may believe that it is more important to love others or that
self-love is selfish. However, if you love others from a place of
no self-love, you are going to end up depleting yourself and
then you will resent others. Resentment can result in negative
treatment toward others and, in its most potent form, results in
the emotion of hatred. It can also lead to self-hatred (which can
be conscious or subconscious). We are meant to be love in the
world, both for ourselves and for others. When we get depleted
and move into resentment, we are no longer aligned with our
spirit or the energy of Divine Love.

Your spirit is connected to and is part of the vast energy
field of eternal consciousness. Some people refer to the field
of eternal consciousness as Big Love, God, the Divine, All
that Is, Unitive Consciousness, or Source. *Big Love* contains a
nourishing and enlivening energy.

All of us are made of energy, and we are connected to the
larger energy of the universe. When we feel love for others or for
ourselves, we are channeling that nourishing enlivening energy.
Alignment with our spirit and opening to the unconditional
love that is there for us can be physically energizing. This flow of
energy from our spirit is always present, we just are not focusing
on it. Consequently, we are not consciously aware of it. This

energy is the nonphysical aspect of ourselves that emerged from the field of eternal consciousness into a physical form on Earth.

Energy medicine practices tap into this revitalizing energy field. There are several ways to experience this energy for yourself. Energy medicine will be discussed more fully in chapter 9. However, here is an exercise to introduce you to an energy practice and to help you with beginning to learn how to tap into the energy flow of spirit.

Try This Exercise: Tapping into the Energy Flow of Spirit

As we did in the previous exercise, begin by taking a long slow breath, bringing all of your awareness to your physical body. Sit quietly and imagine yourself opening to a flow of energy coming down from above your head and filling your body. Imagine that there is an opening at the top of your head. Try imagining that the energy has a color and visualize it or sense it moving into and through your body. Just ask yourself, "If this energy had a color, what color would it be?"

While doing this, take a deep breath all the way down into your belly and then imagine exhaling either down through your legs and feet or out through your heart. Do this in whichever way you feel most drawn to.

A shortcut for this exercise is to follow these steps: sit, breathe out deeply, focus upward, open, breathe in deeply, sense, feel, listen, perceive, receive, expand, and imagine breathing out to the ground.

Once you have completed the exercise, pause and notice what feels different. You may sense a lightness, a tingling, or something else. Take a moment now to journal your answers to these questions.

- What physical sensations did you notice?
- Did the energy have a color? Did the color change or stay the same?
- How did you feel once you completed the exercise?

Giving From a Place of Fullness

It is important to pay close attention to how much energy and love you are giving away and/or is being taken from you. You can unknowingly be depleted by others who make continual requests. Anger and resentment are emotions that can feel energizing, but those emotions can also deplete your energy.

Techniques for clearing and strengthening your energy field, ultimately keeping you from feeling depleted, are described later in chapters 8 and 9.

For now, start by paying close attention to your energy reserves. Doing so will enable you to give from a place of fullness. Let us use the analogy of a battery. At any given time it is helpful to pause and check how much "juice" you have left in your battery. Oftentimes we may be unknowingly operating on less than 50 percent and yet still be pushing ourselves to give more. The lower your battery's charge the harder it can be to get it back to full charge.

If you have more love (energy) flowing out than coming in and you are feeling depleted, it can be more difficult to fully feel the love from your spirit and the support of the Divine. When you truly love yourself by being kind to yourself, monitoring your energy levels, and nurturing yourself (the way you would nurture someone else), you will feel more energized. You will also experience a greater capacity to stay open. When you are more open, you will be more able to fully feel all the love and support of your spirit and Spirit.

If you are still not convinced, just give it a try. "The proof is in the pudding."

Try This Exercise: Bringing In Spirit and "Big Love"

I would like to offer another way in which you can more fully experience the importance of opening up to receive your spirit, and the energy of *Big Love*.

This exercise is best done in a full bathtub of water or in a pool or in some other body of water. I have done this in the ocean, in a pool, and in a bathtub.

Once again, we will begin the exercise by taking a long slow breath, bringing all of your awareness to your physical body. Now, as you are in the bathtub or floating in a body of water, take another long deep breath and notice what happens when you do that. As you breathe the air in, your body rises in the water. You become lighter and more buoyant. Receive the energy, the love, and the abundance that are in the breath.

Now exhale, noticing what happens when you let all of the air out. As you release the air, your body becomes heavier and you sink in the water. Experience the feeling of giving the air away, depleting yourself. Spirit and air enliven you, support you, and lift you up. When you are separate from Spirit and air, you literally begin to sink. Consider this as a meditation. Be in your body and practice opening up and bringing your spirit in, using your breath. Then release the air with an exhale, and feel into the sensation of letting go.

As you do this practice, notice where your awareness wants to go. You may even discover a peaceful feeling in the void between the breaths.

Now take a moment to journal your answers to these questions.

- Did you enjoy this exercise?
- Were you more aware of the feeling of receiving and filling up (inhaling) or of the feeling of releasing and depleting (exhaling)?
- What did you notice in the void?
- What else comes to mind when you think of Spirit and breath as being the same?

Overcoming Self-Love Challenges

If you are someone who finds it challenging to love yourself unconditionally, in addition to the exercise I just described, try paying attention to one thing in the day that you appreciate about yourself. Maybe it is that you made a point to eat a good breakfast, or to go to bed at a decent hour, or to take some quiet time, or to learn something new, or to complete a task, or to do something that was uncomfortable, or to smile at someone who seemed to be having a hard day, or you were able to laugh at something that could have been irritating.

Can you find something, anything, that you like about yourself?

It does not need to be something that is always present. It can be something small at this moment.

Finding something each day that you appreciate about yourself begins to set the stage for self-love, and helps balance out the subconscious negative beliefs and mental programs that are running in the background, out of your awareness. This is not self-centered, narcissistic, or selfish. However, your logical conscious mind may tell you that it is; this is a strategy of the protective personality to stay in control and/or to protect you.

As you name things that you appreciate about yourself, you can begin to feel more self-love. Then you will make more self-loving choices. Choosing to read this book is an act of loving yourself. Choosing to notice your inner dialogue and detach from harsh self-criticism is loving yourself. The more you make self-loving choices, the more you will feel the love of your spirit and of the Divine. The more you feel the love of your spirit and of the Divine, the more you can carry that back out into the world.

We are taught to put others before ourselves. But, if we do not love ourselves first, we will not be bringing our whole self to those we are helping. When we are in the flow of *Big Love*, we will be more able to flow that to others from the place of our own fullness.

Chapter 2

The Interplay Between Your Physical Self and Your Higher Self

The Window of Tolerance and Why It Is Important to Understand

*T*he window of tolerance (WOT) is a concept developed by neuroscientist Dan Siegel to describe an optimal zone of arousal, in which one is able to adequately manage their emotions while engaging with others. When we are in our WOT, there is moderate activation of the sympathetic nervous system (SNS) and the parasympathetic nervous system (PNS). These components of the nervous system (described below), when activating in a balanced way, allow one to maintain engagement with the world in an optimal way. When the fluctuations are too extreme, one is said to be out of their WOT.

In her book *Anchored: How to Befriend Your Nervous System Using Polyvagal Theory*, Deb Dana, a licensed clinical social worker, clinician, and consultant, describes the overactivated SNS as follows:

> *When enlisted in a survival mode, the sympathetic system activates fight and flight, and the hypothalamic-pituitary-adrenal ... axis ... begins to release cortisol and adrenaline.... In addition to this quick, short-term adrenaline-fueled response, the sympathetic system also responds to distress with the release of cortisol. Persistent experiences, like being surrounded by difficult people, living in a place that feels unsafe, or working in an environment that feels toxic, can bring an ongoing cortisol response that feels like a swirl of energy and leaves you in an unending, and unattainable, search for calm.*

Conversely, the PNS includes both the ventral and dorsal branches of the vagus nerve, and when overactivated is described as follows:

> *In this survival mode, the dorsal vagus takes us out of awareness, out of connection and into collapse and immobilization. In this survival state, we feel disconnected and numb and have the experience of being here but not here, and the sense of going through the motions of life without really caring. We suffer with digestive problems as our biological systems move into conservation mode, everything slowing down to maintain just enough energy to keep us alive. We hope that if we disappear, become invisible, and don't feel what's happening or inhabit where we are, we will survive. We escape into not knowing, not feeling and a sense of not being.*

On the other hand, when we are in our WOT, we feel a sense of ease, calm, and safety. When we are in our WOT, we experience mild to moderate fluctuations of SNS upregulation, which prompt us to want to interact with our environment, and mild to moderate fluctuations of PNS downregulation, which prompt us to rest and digest (activating the digestive system). In polyvagal theory, which was developed in the 1990s by Stephen Porges, this state of calm engagement is called "parasympathetic ventral vagal." When we are in our WOT, we feel more able to open up to connect with our own inner experiences, with others, and with our spirit. This is a state in which we can be present with others from a feeling of security and calm. It is a calm connectedness, both internally and externally.

Understanding the WOT and learning how to be in a parasympathetic ventral vagal state have had profoundly positive impacts on my spiritual growth and on the outcomes that my clients have experienced. When I am in a ventral vagal state, open to Spirit, the me that I bring to the world (and the clients whom I serve) is a grounded, calm, joyful, and loving energy.

Anxiety, Depression, and Grief

Let us take this further and consider a different understanding of anxiety, depression, and grief.

Anxiety is a signal to reconnect to the Divine support of the Earth and your breath. What we know from neuroscience is that when we are feeling anxious, the sympathetic nervous system (SNS) is in overdrive. The SNS is the part of the nervous system that regulates the beating of our heart and our breathing, and is designed to protect us and maintain our survival. As the SNS is more activated, the heart rate and respirations speed up. SNS overdrive feels as though you are mashing down on the gas pedal of your car and you feel all revved up. When you feel revved up, you will oftentimes feel more scattered. That scattered feeling is also a signal that things are changing in your energy field.

Remember: you have a field of energy that runs through your body and extends beyond it. This field of energy is your spirit and connects you to the greater energy field of Unitive Consciousness. The embodied life experience involves managing the interface of your energy field with the nervous system that runs through your physical body.

Living on the edge—having an overactive sympathetic nervous system—can also feel like irritability, agitation, fearfulness, edginess, or being overly excited. Some examples of this include when you cannot get to sleep at night because your mind keeps reviewing the events of the day or the things on your to-do list that you did not get done; or when you are at a social gathering and you get the overwhelming feeling to leave; or when you are unexpectedly asked to make a presentation to a group during a meeting with people you have never met before. When we do not realize that these feelings indicate a physical event happening in our nervous system, and are a reflection of what is happening with our energy field, we often will have the tendency to look outside ourselves, to blame someone else or something else for the way we are feeling.

Externalizing what we are experiencing internally is a common reaction that goes back to the basic survival function of the SNS. However, at those times when you are feeling anxious, irritable, fearful, or edgy, if you pause, breathe, and slow down—thereby activating the calming PNS and sending a message to the body that it is safe—then you will give yourself the opportunity to return to a balanced state of feeling more calm.

In the work I have done with clients, the strategies (which are often employed in session) that have proven to be helpful are as follows:

- deep breathing,
- applying pressure to certain pressure points,
- utilizing sensory strategies such as walking barefoot on the earth, digging in the dirt, connecting with a tree,
- using cold water on the base of your neck and forehead,
- wiggling in your chair to feel the contact sensation between your body and the chair,
- squeezing and opening your toes and feet, and
- smelling an Earthy smell (cinnamon, clove, etc.).

While this is not an exhaustive list, I offer it here as a starting place for you to begin experimenting with your unique way of moving from a place of anxiety and SNS overdrive back into a calm regulated state.

Try any of these techniques to see what works best for you. When you look more closely at these strategies, you realize that what you are actually doing is coming back to Spirit. Spirit is in the breath, in the water, in the grass, and in the earth, the dirt. It is your connection to your mind that revs things up and it is your connection to your spirit that slows things back down. When you pause to breathe deeply into your belly and use any of the grounding and calming sensory strategies just described, you are coming home to yourself and to the core of your energy, home to your spirit. Feeling anxious is a signal to ground yourself into the energy of the Earth, which reconnects you to your true Self.

Depression As a Signal to Re-Engage

Now that you better understand what is happening in your nervous system when you are all revved up because of an overactive SNS, let us look at the other side of the spectrum—depression. When you are feeling depressed, depleted, or deflated, your parasympathetic nervous system (PNS) has gone into overdrive. This is the equivalent of mashing on your car's brakes. Experiences, external or internal (including critical verbal and nonverbal experiences), can trigger parasympathetic overdrive leading to depression.

Remember: thoughts lead to feeling states.

When we accept critical statements as truth and we have thoughts that take us to shame, disgust, hopelessness, powerlessness, or guilt, we may feel like crawling into a hole and never coming out—giving up on ourselves and others. When we do not realize that this PNS overdrive is a physical event happening in our nervous system or a reflection of what is happening with our energy field, we often will have the tendency to look outside ourselves, to blame someone else for the way we are feeling.

Some of the strategies that can help bring you back to a feeling of aliveness include these:

- interacting with others,
- smiling,
- watching a funny video or movie,
- playing with an animal,
- helping someone else,
- listening to uplifting music,
- connecting with nature,
- looking up at the sky, and
- engaging in a task or some kind of problem-solving activity (i.e., doing a puzzle).

These strategies can take you to a more light-hearted feeling state. If you do not have close friends or family near you, then you will want to go to places where you are around others (which is the exact opposite of what you will feel like doing). As you use these strategies, you are reactivating the SNS, which is the pathway back to the parasympathetic ventral vagal state and a feeling of connection.

If you are experiencing depression, consider it as a signal to re-engage with your spirit and with others; it is a signal to not give up. When you are depressed, your spirit is still there, calling out to you, saying, "Look this way." If you look up and open up, even if it is just to stretch your arms out and open, you may start to feel the difference.

Remember: You are not meant to be alone and the big T-Truth is that you are never alone.

Your spirit has been with you since the very moment of your existence and knows everything about you; your spirit knows everything you have ever done; it knows everything you have ever said and adores you, loves you, cherishes you, and truly understands you. Your spirit knows those times when you have ever been proud, and those times when you have ever felt ashamed and your spirit loves you; your spirit knows all the choices you have ever made and your spirit loves you.

Your spirit is always with you, even during those times when it does not feel that way to you. Connection with your spirit will bring you back into resonance with the magnificence and brilliance of your true Self. Experiencing challenges can lead to contraction, a pulling in to withdraw from the world. But what if challenges are an opportunity or invitation to expand? You actually cannot know expansion without contraction. It is the nature of the universe.

Grief As a Sign of the Power of Your Heart

Grief is a feeling that naturally occurs when we lose something or someone whom we have deeply loved.

When you make the choice to love, you are making the choice to open your heart. Your spirit calls you to open your heart—to know the power of your heart. Spirit is Divine Love energy and your energy field emerges from the greater field of Love. When you open your heart and connect with others, spirit to spirit, it can be an amazing yet very vulnerable experience.

We are designed to love, but our human psyches, our personalities, may try to avoid or resist that. Fully loving another may not feel safe; it may feel too vulnerable. However, if we go through life avoiding what could be painful, we are not living fully from our spirit. Loving others can be painful. Loving others and then losing them can be devastating.

We are on this human journey to feel, to grow, and to learn lessons. It is why we chose to come here. You are here to know yourself in truth and to bring the brilliance of your spirit to others through relationships, through helping, and through caring. Your spirit is powerful and loving. You are here to be love and light in the world, and that calls for open-hearted living.

Chapter 3

Religions, Varying Beliefs, and Spiritual Practices

*H*elping people recover from religious trauma is a big part of what I do professionally. So I feel it's valuable to explore the difference between being religious, spiritual, atheistic, agnostic, and pluralistic (holding several views at once). I believe that from the higher view of spirit, there is space for all these viewpoints to exist. Whatever your belief system, they are all part of the human journey and our quest for soul growth.

There are thousands of religions in the world, such as Christianity, Judaism, Hinduism, Buddhism, and so forth. Religions can vary from being liberal to being more conservative or fundamentalist. A person may consider themselves religious by culture or by practice and/or by participation with a group. The clients with whom I work with come from many different orientations, including religious but not spiritual; religious and spiritual; spiritual but not religious; atheistic; agnostic; and pluralistic.

Religious

For those who are religious, and have come to me for help, I have found the more dogmatic their religion, the more traumatizing it was for them to be part of that religion. I understand that is a bold statement and it is one that I do NOT make lightly. Formal church, when it is at its best, can be a place of refuge, support, care, and purpose. When people come together as a religious group to support each other and help others, then they are living from their spirit. However, if the accepted beliefs and behaviors of the religious group are not inclusive, uplifting, and affirming, then religious trauma can occur.

Your spirit does not care what religious beliefs you have or do not have, unless your beliefs interfere with knowing your magnificence and your wholeness. If your religion or group focuses on teachings that elicit guilt, shame, and fear (and if you accept those teachings), it will be more difficult for you to connect with and trust your spirit. It will be more difficult for you to believe the big-T Truth of your wholeness, and your divine essence. You will have more tendency to place value outside yourself. You will have more tendency to look for acceptance and approval from a God that is "out there," who you may believe is judging your thoughts and actions.

The more controlling the religious group or organization is, the more unhealthy it is. This can come in the form of rules about who to associate with and which activities are approved. Similarly, the more conditional the religious group or organization is, the more unhealthy it is. This can come in the form of rules about one's sexual orientation and/or marital status. We know this to be true for family relationships; it is the same for a church family and church relationships.

I believe you do not have to do anything to be worthy of God's love. You ARE love and light, and Unitive Consciousness is love and light. Worthiness is not something to reach for or strive for. You are worthy, you are love, you are spirit; there is no separation. Your spirit energy is always flowing to you; Divine Love and light are always flowing to you. It is your natural state.

When I work with clients who have experienced religious trauma, one of the first things we talk about is the difference between healthy and unhealthy guilt. The feeling of guilt is connected to your conscience. When it is working properly, your conscience signals you that you may have just said or done something hurtful or wrong. Your conscience is there to help you navigate the world in a loving way and to signal you to make a repair, in the moment, as needed.

However, if you are taught that to be a good person or to be worthy of love you must control or eliminate thoughts and behaviors that are natural to being human, then you are set up for unhealthy guilt. Unhealthy guilt happens when you go from feeling as though you did something bad to the belief of *I am bad* or *I am unworthy* or *I don't deserve to be loved*.

**Remember: None of these beliefs aligns with
the big-T Truth of who you are.**

You are divine light and love, you are God essence, you are perfect, you are whole. Every human is God embodied. That can become confusing when humans are more in their *humaning* than in their spirit. When a person's human personality is running the show, some pretty unkind things can happen. We are meant to be living from our spirit. It is the human personality that draws us away from our spirit. The more we make thought part of our identity, the more we move away from spirituality. When we are functioning from our personality, our thoughts will often take us to the emotion of fear. Fear is one of the furthest vibrational frequencies away from love, the vibration of God. When we are in fear, we behave to protect ourselves. When we are in a protective state, it closes us off from and separates us from others, and also closes us off from and separates us from our spirit. That is the human condition and the experience we are meant to have.

What if sin were the forgetting of our Oneness? And what if heaven were the inner and outer realms of consciousness? You are here to have these experiences of being pulled away from your spirit and Source, to feel the emotions that happen in those moments, and to find your way back to the Oneness of Unitive Consciousness. The vibration of Source never goes away. It is a matter of returning to the resonance of Oneness.

Religious and Spiritual

To be "religious and spiritual" usually means that you are part of an organized religious group, and you are open to spiritual connection and experiences. Spirituality is about your level of consciousness—the transcendence of your thoughts and beliefs—your willingness to go beyond rational thought. Being religious and spiritual may mean that you place high value on experiencing your connection to spirit.

I would say that I fall in this category. I still go to church from time to time, but mostly I am going to see my church family, people I have known for decades. I go to connect with those I love and to bring the energy of love and light to the group. We are each meant to be love and light in the world, especially in places where others are unsure of their worthiness. I go to plant seeds of the big-T Truth of who we are, as needed. I also go because the vibrational frequency of the music takes me to the vibrational frequency of Spirit. I still enjoy reading the bible on my own, and I focus on what scripture has to say about Spirit.

I have also been studying teachings other than Christianity, including Buddhism and Hinduism. Most Christian religions do not believe in reincarnation; but I do. Hinduism most aligns with the research on reincarnation. Whatever the religion is, I am drawn to the teachings that are inclusive, unconditional, and non-shaming.

Elaine Pagels's book, *The Gnostic Gospels*, describes early Christians who were both religious and spiritual. The gnostics refuted the authority of the Roman Church and saw the spiritual experience of connection to Jesus as valuable and real.

I have found the writings of Richard Rohr of the Center for Action and Contemplation to be especially helpful because of his nondualistic approach. He is a Catholic priest who challenges the unhealthy patterns that have developed over the years in many organized religions. In his daily meditation messages, he has stated that the "Great Truth" is loving, joyful, and inclusive.

I find the practice of contemplative prayer to be in the category of both religious and spiritual. In general, I strive to stay focused on what is good versus what is evil. I stay focused on moving toward the energy of well-being versus judgment. I am sometimes not sure where I would categorize myself, and I am not sure that it really matters.

More Spiritual than Religious

To be more spiritual than religious simply means that you are not attaching your spiritual beliefs or spiritual growth to a religious group or norm. Throughout the years, I have been drawn to teachers who speak about and focus on the human connection to the energy of the cosmos and Universal Consciousness—our eternal existence. Some of these teachers have included Ernest Holmes, Eckhart Tolle, Deepak Chopra, Esther Hicks (who channels Abraham), Sonia Choquette, Wayne Dyer, Thich Nhat Hanh, Elaine Pagels, Michael Singer, Jack Kornfield, and Richard Rohr. While some of these teachers also have been or are religious, they acknowledge the importance of the spiritual practice of opening up to the wholeness of who you are and feeling your connection to All That Is.

Learning from teachers who focus on Spirit, Oneness, wholeness, Universal Consciousness, and vibration has led me to practices that feel empowering and aligned with the truth of who I am. The pivotal book that started my journey into spirituality was *The Power of Now: A Guide to Spiritual Enlightenment* by Eckhart Tolle. I was made aware of this book by a client who had been struggling with chronic anxiety. He reported that his anxiety completely changed when he incorporated the concepts from *The Power of Now* into his life. Over the years, many of my clients have found this to be true. Until I read Tolle's book, I had no idea how much I was never in the *now* moment. I was completely unaware that my thoughts (and my energy) were constantly moving between rehashing the past or anticipating the future. Once I became aware of what was happening in my mind and found peace in the present moment, I was more able to connect to my spirit.

Another pivotal moment in my journey from religious to spiritual was when I learned about Ernest Holmes and his book, *The Science of Mind*. This broadened my childhood perspective of God beyond the image of the white man with the long gray beard. For me, the teachings of Ernest Holmes bridge religion and spirituality.

Other Practices

I'd like to offer a brief description of several practices I have learned from teachers whom I consider to be spiritual. These are powerful practices that I use personally and regularly share with my clients.

The Emotional Guidance Scale

This practice is taught by Esther Hicks and Abraham. The Emotional Guidance Scale denotes particular vibrational frequencies using everyday words that describe emotions. The scale itself can be found using a Google search, and in the book, *Ask and It Is Given: Learning to Manifest Your Desires* by Esther and Jerry Hicks. According to Abraham, each emotion listed on the scale is an indicator of the degree to which you are or are not allowing full alignment or openness to the flow of Source energy. The more you are in alignment with and open to Source, the higher your vibrational frequency. The higher vibrational frequencies are further up the scale. Each place on the scale has some feeling words to describe its particular vibration frequency.

For this practice and process, the words themselves are less important than the feeling associated with the frequency. The goal is to work with the feelings and the vibrations. When you are "up the scale," you are most aligned with your spirit. When you are "down the scale," you are closed off to your spirit, and whatever thoughts you are having are not how your spirit sees it.

Try This Exercise: Changing Your Vibrational Frequency

As always, begin by taking a long slow breath, bringing all of your awareness to your physical body. Now take a moment to look at an emotional scale chart (a variety of scales are available online and can be accessed by googling "emotional guidance scale") and decide which word best describes your current vibrational state. Then, notice any thoughts you are currently having that correlate with that vibrational frequency, that emotion. Now, look at the chart again and choose a higher place on the scale that you would like to move toward. Choose a thought that would correlate with that vibrational frequency, that emotion. Practice that thought and see if another thought comes in that is also at that higher vibrational frequency.

Take slow easy breaths and stay open. Gaze upward. Stay curious.

Once you feel you are at that higher vibrational frequency, look at the scale again. Decide if you would like to continue working your way up to a higher frequency. If so, repeat the process. As you start accessing higher vibrational frequencies, feel the momentum building. Be patient and stay curious.

Now take a moment to journal your answers to the following questions.

- Where was your starting point on the scale?
- Were you able to make any progress with moving up the scale?
- How difficult or easy was it for you?
- Did you try it with a specific issue or did you use general statements/thoughts?

Staying mindful of my vibrational frequency on a moment-by-moment basis has been an incredibly empowering experience. It has proven to me that I am the one responsible for how I feel and for the experiences that show up in my life. When I start having more negative encounters in the world, I pause to check my vibration. As I stay mindful of my vibrational frequency and remember to reach for thoughts that will take me to higher vibrational frequencies, life just naturally feels more magical. All of the inspirations for this book came to me during those moments of being in the expansive higher vibration of my spirit.

Over the years I have encouraged my clients to use this powerful tool. Often, in session, we will work together on thoughts that will shift their vibrational frequency. Once the frequency begins to shift, accessing higher vibrational thoughts becomes easier.

There are countless YouTube videos that explain all of the processes taught by Abraham through Esther Hicks. I have found that listening to these short videos also shifts my vibrational frequency.

Movement

Movement can be a spiritual practice. This may include dancing, shaking, bouncing, qigong, or moving in any way that gets you out of your thoughts and into your body. When you move your body, you are simultaneously enlivening your energy field. When you enliven your energy field and bring your awareness to the physical sensations, you are moving into the vibration of your spirit. After moving your body for about three to four minutes, see if you can then connect to a lighter emotion, feeling, vibrational frequency. All of this movement is even more powerful if you also incorporate deep breathing and consciously set the intention of opening to the energy of the universe.

Nineteen Possible Solutions

I learned this practice of listing nineteen possible solutions from Sonia Choquette, an intuitive with whom I have studied for years. The practice is best used when you are in a lower vibrational frequency due to a problem that needs solving. First, make a list of nineteen possible solutions to the problem you are having. Be sure to include solutions that would take you out of your comfort zone, not just the "safe" solutions. Have fun with the exercise, and really think outside the box. What really makes this exercise powerful is the condition that these are not solutions or actions that you are committing to do. You are simply generating ideas as a way to reveal more options.

After you have completed the list, review each solution you came up with. Taking the initiative to do the exercise, in and of itself, will shift your energy enough that you will see the direction to take. It also makes space for your spirit to speak to you and support you in your problem-solving. It really does work!

Here's an example of how this worked for a client of mine who had been struggling with marriage problems for a long time. He still loved his wife but was very unhappy in the marriage. He came up with the following nineteen possible solutions.

1. Discuss divorce.
2. Move out and get my own place but stay married.
3. Ask her to move out.
4. Sleep in separate rooms.
5. Get divorced.
6. Make staying in the relationship conditional on going to counseling.
7. Have an affair.
8. Propose an open marriage.
9. Go on the vacation we wanted to take several years ago.
10. Propose weekly dates.
11. Stop looking for her to do things that make me feel good.
12. Go live with my brother and his family for a while.
13. Take the job at the branch that would require us to live apart for a while.

14. Start speaking up more.

15. Be more honest about how I'm feeling.

16. Figure out things that I can do to be happier myself.

17. Focus on positive experiences with the kids.

18. Ask my friend's wife to talk to her.

19. Accept our marriage as it is.

This client had no desire to leave his marriage, but also was feeling miserable with the current conditions of the relationship. Doing this exercise freed him up to consider the many alternatives available to him. When he was energetically open to leaving, he became more aware of how he was not asserting his needs. It was as though his spirit said to him, "You deserve to be happy and it is up to you to make that happen."

Hypnosis and Spirituality

Doing hypnosis that involves going to the spiritual realm has naturally led me to more exploration of spirituality, belief systems, and their influences. I am continually amazed at the many ways in which people are drawn to do past life regressions (PLR) and Life Between Lives (LBL) regressions. (I have explained about PLRs in chapter 1.) It is interesting to hear each client's beliefs and to see how they respond to the regressions.

An LBL regression is a specific type of hypnotherapy that enables you to travel to your soul state and feel supported by loving energies or entities in the nonphysical spiritual realm. (LBL hypnotherapy is discussed in detail in chapter 6.)

It is curious to me when those who are atheistic (who do not believe in the existence of a divine being or beings) pursue an LBL. The afterlife still holds curiosity for them. I have come to think that maybe their spirit is whispering to them. I have found that those who are agnostic (not sure of what exists beyond the physical) are very much able to get answers and to get clarity through their LBL experience.

What is obvious to me is that we are all on some sort of a spiritual path. Consciously or unconsciously, we are just trying to figure it all out, trying to get to a good feeling place, trying to get some clarity, returning home to the big-T Truth of who we are. In chapters 5 and 6, I provide case studies that demonstrate how clients are able to clear out and release faulty beliefs through PLR and LBL regression.

Be Open and Curious

When it comes to your beliefs, consider giving yourself permission to be open and curious about all of the teachings. We each incarnate with our own spiritual gifts to share. Maybe a metaphor for this would be a spiritual buffet. Do you really want to explore just one part of the buffet? There were many prophets in the past and there are many prophets in the world now. As I have broadened my exploration, I have had amazing insights that I am pretty sure I would not have had if I only allowed myself to think about the teachings of Christianity.

**Remember: you always have the freedom
to choose what you want your journey to be.
From the viewpoint of spirit, it is all good.**

Dualism versus Nondualism

Dualism is the division of something conceptually into two opposing or contrasting aspects. Dualism results in black and white thinking, right and wrong thinking. Many religions embrace and even insist on dualistic beliefs. These beliefs inevitably result in the exclusion of those who do not fully embrace the beliefs. By contrast, nondualism supports the ideas of oneness and no separation. With nonduality is the belief that everything and everyone in the universe is one. There is no exclusion.

Hinduism and Buddhism include the philosophy and teaching of nondual consciousness, as do Christian contemplative practices and mysticism. For a very thorough understanding of these concepts, I recommend the writings of Richard Rohr.

The ideas, concepts, and beliefs that I am putting forward in this book come from the perspective of nondualism. I believe that Spirit loves and includes everyone, regardless of their beliefs.

I am reminded of Ed Young's children's book, *Seven Blind Mice*, based on an Indian fable. The fable has several versions. Young's story goes like this. Six blind mice each explore some aspect of the same elephant. The first mouse explores the elephant's leg and concludes that the elephant is a pillar. The second mouse explores the elephant's trunk and concludes that the elephant is a snake. The third mouse explores the elephant's tusk and concludes that the elephant is a spear. The fourth mouse explores the top of the elephant's head and concludes that the elephant is a great cliff. The fifth mouse explores the elephant's ear and concludes that the elephant is a fan. The sixth mouse explores the elephant's tail and concludes that the elephant is a rope. Each of these six mice has its own truth.

In reality, they are all only looking at part of the picture. The seventh mouse explores the elephant from end to end, top to bottom, and reveals the wisdom of knowing the whole truth. I believe we are called to see the whole elephant and to do so we need to be open and inclusive with our beliefs and with our treatment of each other.

We are all part of the Divine, regardless of the religious group that we may or may not be part of. Endorsing beliefs that result in others being seen as *less than* is not aligned with Spirit.

Reincarnation

What if this life you are living is just one of many? I never used to pay attention to the idea of reincarnation. I had a vague idea that it was something other religions believed in. I formed an opinion early in life that the idea of reincarnation did not matter much to me, one way or the other.

Then in my fifties, as I said, I had the several opportunities to experience a past life during large group regression sessions, one of which was with Dr. Brian Weiss. He is the author of *Many Lives, Many Masters: The True Story of a Prominent Psychiatrist, His Young Patient, and the Past-Life Therapy That Changed Both Their Lives.*

Following those experiences, I read about past lives and LBL regressions in Michael Newton's books, *Journey of Souls* and *Destiny of Souls*. While reading the details he presents, I had the strange and overwhelming feeling that I was re-remembering things I already knew; it was a sort of déjà vu. I did not know what to make of that feeling, but I knew it was important.

Even though I had seen myself in other lifetimes when I did the past life regression (PLR) sessions, a part of me was still skeptical. My logical mind had convinced me that I was making those stories up. My belief in the reality of past lives changed dramatically when I discovered that reincarnation has been studied and researched. Yes, you read that right. Reincarnation has been researched for years, and actually is not something to just muse about as an interesting idea.

I first learned about the research into reincarnation when I read Cathy Byrd's book, *The Boy Who Knew Too Much: An Astounding True Story of a Young Boy's Past-Life Memories*. This woman who was raised a Christian tells about her experience of discovering that her son had been Major League Baseball player, Lou Gehrig, in a previous life. Since I was raised in the Christian faith, I found it very helpful to read about how Cathy Byrd had the courage to open up to the idea of reincarnation, an idea that is not accepted in traditional Christianity.

For help for her son, Byrd describes how she contacted Dr. Jim Tucker, a child psychiatrist and Professor of Psychiatry and Neurobehavioral Sciences at the University of Virginia School of Medicine. Dr. Tucker was raised in the Southern Baptist Convention and had published a book titled, *Return to Life: Extraordinary Cases of Children Who Remember Past Lives*. This book summarizes the cases Dr. Tucker studied using rigorous scientific methodology.

I am sharing this information so you can learn for yourself about this research.

In *The Boy Who Knew Too Much*, Byrd provides the details of her work with Dr. Tucker as well as her experience of having a PLR. She describes her PLR experience, the impact of the PLR on her life, and the steps she took following her PLR to track down confirmation of the details she had received during the regression. She describes a series of discoveries that she made, as a result; these discoveries confirmed her experiences in her PLR.

This evidence was not only fascinating to me, but it completely convinced me of the importance of recognizing the existence of every one of our lifetimes.

Some others who have researched and written about the phenomenon of past lives include psychologists Helen Wambach, PhD, Peter Ramster, and psychiatrist Ian Stevenson, MD.

Most of the individuals who contact me for PLR or LBL regression work are seeking to relieve some form of suffering, including grief associated with the loss of a loved one by suicide, intense chronic anxiety, a sense of feeling lost, and relief from a physical affliction. Many of them have tried other more traditional avenues of relief and are still experiencing some form of suffering or distress. However, some are more in a place of pure curiosity.

Does it matter whether or not you believe in past lives? Do you have to believe in past lives to benefit from undergoing a PLR or LBL? The answer to both of those questions is no. Whether or not you do believe in past lives, there are ways in which experiences in other lifetimes can continue to impact you in your current life.

In *Untying the Karmic Knot*, psychotherapist Diane Morrin presents numerous case studies documenting this effect. As Morrin says,

> *Past-life regression provides access to the source of our emotional, physical, and spiritual problems. Through a hypnotherapeutic journey to an earlier time and place, we experience the inciting event or relationship. That experience releases the tension tightening the Karmic*

Knot. Comprehension cuts the thread, as it unravels the
burden carried by us from the past into the present.

If you are having struggles (physical, mental, emotional, or spiritual) in your current incarnation, some aspect may be tied to a past life. When that happens, it is necessary to unravel and shift the energetic connection to the past life in order to clear it in your current life. This is where past life regression, quantum healing, and energy medicine can be especially helpful. These healing modalities address the multidimensional being that you are.

Choosing to come to planet Earth is a big choice. It is a big deal. It is a big project. You did not make this choice lightly. You set a plan before you came. You chose the lessons and the main and supporting characters for your project. You likely came back to correct some of your previous experiences from other lifetimes and to pick up where you left off with your lessons and your growth. You came to continue your learning and to grow more, but you also came to have joy, ease, and fun.

I remind myself daily to remember the ease, remember the joy, remember the fun. That is my connection back to my brilliance and the energy of my spirit.

Your spirit is expansive, open, and free. Your spirit is your connection to the energy of Divine Love. So we cycle between spirit and human. We are spirit poured into and grounded in this physical body. When you simultaneously stay grounded in your body and open to your spirit, then you are living an embodied life. As you Stand in Your Brilliance and live an embodied, spirit-guided life, you can channel Divine Love to others, and this ultimately will change the world.

We are here to learn, to teach, to experience sensations and emotions, and to love.

Chapter 4

Healing As a Way of Opening to Your Wholeness

*T*he truth is there is more to you than your human self and you have a spirit that is pure joy, love, and light. Your spirit is your brilliance. Your spirit is beautiful, perfect, a bright light. It is the spark inside you that makes you want to sing, dance, create, laugh, and love. Your spirit is an energetic aspect of you that is connected to the energy of the universe. When you experience a sensation of lightness and expansiveness, you are in a higher vibrational frequency. In that state of expansiveness you are in the vibrational frequency of joy. Joy is love in action. When you are in the vibrational frequency of joy you are bringing your light and love to the world. You are standing in your brilliance.

Try This Exercise: Feeling the Energy of Joy

As always, begin by taking a long slow breath, bringing all of your awareness to your physical body. As you bring your awareness to your physical body, notice the sensation of where your body comes into contact with whatever you are sitting or standing on. Take a few more slow deep breaths in through your nose and out through your mouth. In this moment, as you pause and breathe, see if you can feel into this expansive state of joy. Now take two more deep breaths, but even more slowly. Then, raise your arms above your head, forming the shape of a V. Take one more really long slow breath and when you exhale, imagine that your energy field is rippling out into the universe. Let it expand more and more. Notice any sensation of lightness or expansiveness. You are opening to the energy of your spirit and to the energy of the universe. Close your eyes and feel the joy that is available to you there.

Now take a few moments to journal your answers to the following questions.

- How expansive is your energy?
- Did you feel your energy continuing to expand?
- Did images come into your mind's eye?
- What do you want to remember from this exercise?

When and how do we lose touch with our spirit? How is it that we forget this truth about who we are? To a large extent, forgetting is the outcome of our conditioning and cultural norms that have been passed down for generations. There is a conditioning that happens in your early grade school years.

Imagine for a minute that you see some young children playing together, say maybe in a sandbox. They are enjoying themselves, laughing, exploring, digging, and pouring the sand. Do you think to yourself or say to those children, "You had better get busy, get to work, stop goofing off." Of course not. We accept that the job of a child is to play. We accept that children are meant to have joy. In fact, many of us feel joy just by watching children play.

When we are given opportunities to be in a safe environment, free to play, we are aligned with our spirit and in a place of joy. But as children get older, expectations change. There is a societal agreement that at some point we need to become "responsible." Being responsible is serious business. We are conditioned to believe that being good means you do your chores, get your homework done, and get a job. In fact, children who stay childlike longer, who stay in their imagination and march to the beat of their own drum (as known as their spirit), are often seen as odd, different, and maybe even difficult.

I can tell you that oftentimes, when I was young, if I was fully in my spirit I would get the message (either verbally or nonverbally) that I was too much. Over time, I began to stifle my spirit, to make myself smaller so as not to overwhelm others. While this pleased others, it simultaneously took me out of the vibration of joy and I developed a more serious approach to life.

The challenge is how to become responsible and not lose touch with the joy. It IS possible to be responsible and stay in touch with your joy, with your spirit. Your spirit is always calling you back to the place of joy.

That calling, later in life, can feel like a tug to develop some hobbies. I often will ask my clients early on in our work together, "What brings you joy?" The ways in which we experience joy are as varied as we are as individuals. For some, it is solitary activities like reading, sewing, hiking in nature. For others it's social activities like playing tennis or basketball, coffee with friends.

What is your unique way of feeling joy? Gardening? Hiking? Drawing? Writing? Riding your horse? Learning? (Note: this does not include behaviors that are mind-numbing or emotionally numbing.) What takes you to the place of lightness and expansiveness? How often do you do these things? What might it be like to do that more?

And then I will ask them, "What were you told about being responsible?" It is not uncommon for a client to say that being responsible was just what was expected.

Consider your journey and your experience. How did this play out for you? What were the messages that you received about being responsible? Did your caregivers support you in a way that provided the space for you to be joyful and childlike?

When we step into joy we step out of the drama, challenges, and struggles of the human experience, and open to our whole selves.

Try This Exercise: Finding Joy

As always, begin by taking a long slow breath, bringing all of your awareness to your physical body. Now, take a moment to answer some of these questions in your journal.

- What brings you joy?
- How often do you do that?
- What were the messages you received in your family about being responsible?
- Write a statement of commitment to yourself, a specific plan for how you will bring more joy back into your life.

The Pathway to Joy

For many people, the transition from the freedom and joy of childhood into responsibility was difficult and maybe even painful. You may never have had the opportunity to be free and playful. Play, creativity, and imagination are gateways to your spirit. But what if that was not your life experience? Even if you did not have that opportunity previously, you can still access it now.

A few years ago, on my sixty-first birthday, I received an Ariel Clamshell Bubble Wand as a gift. This wand was fourteen inches long. Not only did it blow bubbles but it lit up. I loved it! After opening this gift, while still in the restaurant, I turned it on in the middle of the restaurant and started waving it around. It brought smiles to so many faces, including mine.

It is so important to give yourself permission to be silly, to let go of being serious, and to allow yourself to be childlike. When was the last time you danced? Skipped? Built a fort? Swung on a swing? Played with bubbles?

If you take time to do these things, you will automatically start to smile. The act of smiling, in and of itself, is beneficial. When you smile, your brain releases serotonin, endorphins, and dopamine. This then can shift you out of feelings of anxiety and depression.

Everyone has their own way of getting to a place of joy. For you, it may be solving a scientific inquiry or finishing a jigsaw puzzle. Completing a difficult task releases endorphins and can take you into a place of joy. Opening to your spirit means doing whatever takes you to a place of lightness and expansiveness.

Whether you are sixteen or sixty, think about how often you were given the message to be more responsible. Especially in American culture, we are rushed to grow up so early. It is important to not take yourself too seriously. You can be responsible *and* joyful. If it was unsafe to be a playful child growing up, now is your chance to recapture that for yourself.

I look around for examples of people being playful in the world. When I see road crews with their bulldozers and levelers I wonder to myself if they have figured out the perfect solution for how to balance responsibility (providing for themselves and their families) with playing in the dirt, so to speak.

Not all of us have a job or profession that aligns with our spirit. If we do not find joy and purpose in our work, then it is even more important to find that in our free time.

I am blessed to live very close to an elementary school. Sitting on my porch and listening to the kids playing on the playground makes me smile, and it reminds me of the importance of play.

Take time to consider these questions about what makes you smile.

- Listening to music?
- Watching a funny show?
- Being with others?
- Being in nature?
- Looking at art?
- Travel?
- Cooking?

There are no right or wrong answers. It is your personal path to joy.

We come into the physical realm (our lives) to learn lessons for our soul growth, and sometimes these lessons are painful. But, the purpose of life is also to live from your spirit and to experience joy. It sounds so simple. Your logical mind will dispute this simple truth, because moving into joy equates to moving out of fear and that is a threat to the protective logical mind. So just consider, what if it were true? What if the purpose of life were joy? How would it feel to try that on as a way of going through the world?

When you recognize that you are spirit, then you realize you are joy. So, if the purpose of life is joy and you are joy, then, the purpose of life is to be you, open to your spirit. To be all of you. Once you open to your spirit, you can tap into the creative energy of the universe. It is from this place that artists of all kinds, including you, create the life you were meant to have.

Alignment

The term *alignment* is frequently used by spiritual teachers, but I feel it is a misnomer. To me, the term *alignment* implies that your spirit is something that is separate from you. I think of alignment differently—as opening up to a part of us that is always present. One way of thinking about alignment is to consider what we are being most influenced by. Because the human journey is messy, it can be difficult to be in joy, to be in our spirit.

The main things that take us out of alignment are thoughts connected to past negative experiences, current negative experiences, and fears about the future. When our minds are focused on negative events and fears, we are led away from openness and into contraction. The question to ask yourself is, "What am I being most influenced by?" We can tell by how we feel. If we are being mostly influenced by our faulty beliefs, then we are aligning with our mind in the form of those faulty beliefs about ourselves and the world. If we are being mostly influenced by negative memories of past experiences or fears about the future, then we are also aligning with our mind. When we align with our minds, we will experience more disturbance inside of ourselves, more tension. This may come in the form of worry, guilt, shame, fear, or deflation, to name a few.

If, however, we are aligning with our breath, with nature, with what is happening in the moment and the sensory experiences of sound, light, color, smells, flavors, and with thoughts of the big-T Truth of who we are, then we are opening to our spirit and standing in our brilliance.

Even in the midst of difficult times or experiences, when we pause and open to our spirit, we will experience more peace, satisfaction, and pleasure. That is how we can transcend the conditioning of the human experience.

> **Remember: It is not about transcending the human experience. Rather, it is about transcending the *conditioning* of the human experience.**

Understanding the Multidimensional You

Much has been written and studied about the human energy field. The field of traditional Chinese medicine is founded on the principle of energy. In Howard Batie's book, *Healing Body, Mind & Spirit: A Guide to Energy-Based Healing*, he states the following.

> *The Human Energy Field (HEF) can be described in terms of three different perspectives: (1) the major and minor chakras throughout the body, (2) the subtle energy fields or energy bodies that surround the physical body, and (3) the energy meridians within the physical body that provide the means of circulating and distributing energy (prana, chi, ki, etc.) to the tissues and organs of the body.*

In Donna Eden's book, *The Little Book of Energy Medicine: The Essential Guide to Balancing Your Body's Energies*, she states this.

> *Energy animates every cell and organ in your body. It is the Life Force and, put simply: when you have it, you are alive; when you don't, you aren't. Your*

body's relationship to this essential energy of nature has been evolving for millions of years. The energies that govern the way your body functions direct your immune system, hormones, and everything else that keeps you alive as decisively as a magnet will organize iron filings into distinct patterns. These energies have an amazing intelligence. They are much smarter than your intellect in keeping you healthy and in repairing you if you become ill. That said, you can mobilize your energies to keep your body and mind humming at their best.

The electrical and electromagnetic aspects of our energy field can be measured with scientific instruments. However, instrumentation that can directly measure the subtle energy fields has not yet been developed. As I looked at various models and theories describing the subtle energy fields or energies bodies, I found some minor discrepancies between descriptions. In general, though, there seems to be a consensus that we have a physical energy body, an etheric energy body, an emotional energy body, a mental energy body, and then one or more spiritual energy bodies.

The densest form of your energy field is your physical energy body. The etheric energy body runs through your physical body and extends beyond your physical body. The emotional energy body is the field just beyond the etheric field. The mental energy body is the energy field just beyond the emotional field and closest to your spiritual energy bodies.

In my early years as a psychotherapist, I was primarily focused on healing modalities that targeted an individual's behaviors, cognitions, and emotions. Studies have shown changes in brain activity and the nervous system of the physical energy body when we experience different emotional phenomena. More recently, the field of mental health has moved toward therapies based on discoveries in the field of neurobiology and focused on regulation of the nervous system.

The field of mindfulness has extended the focus beyond the physical, emotional, and mental energy bodies to the energy field of greater consciousness—to the spiritual energy bodies. When you begin to understand who you are as a multidimensional being and you open up to mindfulness practices and energy medicine practices, you can start to tap into the expanded being that you are. I present more specifics about mindfulness practices and energy medicine practices in chapters 9 and 10.

In summary, any negative beliefs, thoughts, and stories you are storing in your mental energy body can create a block in the connection to your spirit. The mental energy body is the layer directly adjacent to the spiritual energy bodies. The key to having a clear connection to your spirit and to standing in your brilliance is to recognize and shift any negative beliefs about yourself and others.

This can be done in a variety of ways including these:

- psychologically and mentally (using psychotherapy, hypnotherapy, trauma therapy, and/or mindfulness meditation);
- physically (using body work, acupuncture, sound healing therapies, qigong, herbal medicine, naturopathic medicine, and/or yoga); and
- energetically (using quantum techniques, breath work, energy clearing, energy healing techniques, and/or tapping).

We are made up of many energy layers, and the above-mentioned techniques provide multilayer healing. It has taken me years to embrace and acknowledge this reality. Regardless of what you focus on or whatever order you embrace your healing, it will benefit you. I can tell you from my personal healing experience that the most healing came from acknowledging and addressing all the layers.

Over the years, I have known and worked with highly intuitive healers who are connected to their spirit but still struggle with anxiety and depression. If that is your experience, it could be a sign that there are negative beliefs and stories still active in your emotional, mental, or spiritual layers. What I have observed in myself and my clients is that when false beliefs are shifted in the mental field, one can more readily access one's spirit.

Keeping the mental layer clear requires daily attention. You want to attend to the mental layer the same way you attend to your physical health, by being as consistent as possible. Anxiety can also be a sign that more energy is dropping into your field. In that case, it is even more important to break out of the story of your human experience to discover more—your soul, your energy field, expansiveness, freedom, fun, inspiration.

Your spirit holds the true view of you—the whole, worthy, perfect, pure love brilliant you that you are.

My healing journey has included traditional psychotherapy, trauma therapy, body work, sound healings, multiple types of energy healing, past life and life between lives hypnotherapy, quantum healing work, daily breath work, qigong, yoga, prayer, and meditation. (All of these healing approaches are described in more detail in later chapters.)

The healing modalities I sought have been specific to the body I chose and the life experiences I have had. Your healing journey could be quite different. Whatever approach you choose, know that you are on the road back to your wholeness.

On this human journey, we are each a work in progress, not to be confused with being a fix-it-up project. You are NOT a fix-it-up project!

This journey is meant to lead you toward growth. If you have been doing personal growth work for a long time, it can be easy to fall into a mindset of feeling broken. We are all learning lessons and moving toward growth, even when it does not look or feel that way. Some of you may have intentionally chosen a more difficult path for this incarnation. It is important to approach your personal growth from the perspective of self-acceptance and self-understanding versus self-improvement. If you allow them to be, negative experiences can be learning opportunities. I believe that struggle is meant to serve us and lead us toward growth. Perfection is NOT the goal. The natural outcome of self-acceptance and self-understanding is growth and expansion.

It is useful to see ourselves as being like trees. We are each our own unique tree, with our own beautiful markings and characteristics. As we go through challenges we have the opportunity to grow our roots deeper and deeper. When there is limited water, the roots of a tree will grow deep into the ground and spread wide in search of water. When our roots grow deeper, we are then more able to sway in the breeze without being uprooted (this equates to being more flexible). The breeze adds variety and contrast, which can lead to more growth. Your brilliance is always present, even in the "stormy" conditions of life.

Recognizing the Influences of Your Personality

We are here to be spirit embodied (in a body). Bringing the larger part of you, your expanded consciousness, into a human body is a choice. We make this choice to have the human experience for the purpose of growth and the greater purpose of expansion of the universe. We are also here to experience the playground of planet Earth, and to have the emotional experiences that are inherently part of being human. We are meant to experience and find joy. Finding joy is always possible. Even in the midst of hard lessons, there is beauty to be found.

An integral part of the human journey is the development of your personality. You simply cannot leave your personality at the door. Because of this, I encourage my clients to develop a deeper understanding of their personality. The more you understand your personality, the easier it will be for you to realize when your personality is leading and when you are allowing your spirit to lead you. If your personality is running the show to an unhealthy degree, there is more likelihood of experiencing pain, frustration, and judgment (of yourself and others). Understanding your personality enables you to be more consciously aware of what is influencing your perceptions, interpretations, and responses.

When you are in your spirit you will be more open, flexible, and accepting than when you are operating from an unhealthy aspect of your personality. When you are going through the world from the unhealthy aspects of your personality you will be more judgmental, opinionated, and insecure. When you understand yourself better, you are more able to overcome the inner barriers you have and to see your strengths and gifts.

Are you willing to be curious about yourself and how your early childhood experiences impacted you?

The personality typology system that I prefer is called the Enneagram. The Enneagram has become better known in recent years. In fact, there are now a myriad of Enneagram YouTube videos about the nine different Enneagram types. The names of the nine types as used by some Enneagram experts are as follows:

Type 1: the reformer,
Type 2: the helper,
Type 3: the achiever,
Type 4: the individualist,
Type 5: the investigator,
Type 6: the loyalist,
Type 7: the enthusiast,
Type 8: the challenger, and
Type 9: the peacemaker.

The modern Enneagram originates from spiritual wisdom derived from many different ancient traditions including Christianity, Buddhism, Islam, and Judaism. It is a psychological system of understanding personality that is also based on the understanding that we are spiritual beings in a physical world.

The primary objective of the Enneagram is to enhance self-knowledge. The importance of this self-knowledge is emphasized at the very beginning of *The Wisdom of the Enneagram: The Complete Guide to Psychological and Spiritual Growth for the Nine Personality Types* by Don Richard Riso and Russ Hudson when they say the following.

Without self-knowledge, we will not get very far on our spiritual journey, nor will we be able to sustain whatever progress we have made. One of the great dangers of transformational work is that the ego attempts to sidestep deep psychological work by leaping into the transcendent too soon.... Real self-knowledge is an invaluable guardian against such self-deception. The Enneagram takes us places (and makes real progress possible) because it starts working from where we actually are. As much as it reveals the spiritual heights that we are capable of attaining, it also sheds light clearly and nonjudgmentally on the aspects of our lives that are dark and unfree. If we are going to live as spiritual beings in the material world, then these are the areas we most need to explore.

If you are going to live a life aligned with your spirit, it is necessary to recognize patterns that take you out of alignment. If you choose to do the Enneagram, I recommend the RHETI test that is available at enneagraminstitute.com. The Enneagram Institute was founded by Don Richard Riso and Richard Hudson, two of the main modern writers, developers, and scholars of the Enneagram. Once you have identified your Enneagram type, you can obtain a wealth of information to help you with the unique challenges that you are facing in your life.

In *The Wisdom of the Enneagram*, you will find a chart for each type, which describes what is considered healthy, average, and unhealthy for that type. I find this very helpful as a general guide to recognize when a person is or is not moving toward growth. There is much to explore with the Enneagram and the resources available from the institute. There is also a way to explore relationship dynamics between yourself and your partner, based on each of your typologies.

It is very important to remember that examining your personality is not about diagnosis or finding fault with yourself or others. Rather, it is about understanding and accepting yourself and others. Fully understanding all aspects of your personality enables you to shift old patterns that interfere with opening to your magnificence. When you are in a place of self-understanding and self-acceptance you will also begin to react to others with less judgment. You will become more curious about others' behaviors, needs, and attitudes.

The most powerful way to go through life is from a place of curiosity. Just like the young child who is seeing a caterpillar for the first time. Curiosity enables you to experience the world from the more expanded state of your spirit. In this expanded state you can be more detached. *Detachment* simply means acceptance of what is, without an agenda, and letting go of picking sides or needing to win. You are honoring the deeper knowing that everyone is on their own path, here to learn their individual lessons.

We each have the freedom to choose our own path. Being aware of attachments is the beginning of awakening.

Chapter 5

Clearing Conscious and Subconscious Negative Beliefs

Hypnosis and Hypnotherapy

*H*ypnosis is specifically designed to target and undo unhealthy and/or limiting subconscious beliefs. The process of hypnosis involves using an induction, progressive relaxation, and a tone and cadence of the voice in ways that allow you to relax and slow down your brain wave activity. During hypnosis, as you relax, your brain goes into what are called "theta" brainwaves. Access to subconscious beliefs and information occurs when your brain is in theta. Theta brain waves are slower than the beta brain waves that coincide with wakefulness and alertness, and faster than the delta waves that occur during deep sleep. Alpha brain waves coincide with a meditative state.

So far, I have only talked about the conscious and sub-conscious mind. Remember that the conscious mind is your critical reasoning, thinking, and planning mind; it is also the part of your mind that wants to keep you safe. The conscious mind moves back and forth between replaying information and scenes from the past and anticipating what might occur in the future. The subconscious mind is the layer of consciousness holding the beliefs that formed very early in life. It is the layer of the mind that is accessed during hypnosis to change behaviors (such as smoking or overeating), to alter responses, as well as to address trauma from earlier in current and/or previous lifetimes. Hypnosis is especially helpful for changing self-sabotaging behaviors and for removing blockages to fully internalizing affirmations.

A common practice that is taught in personal development programs is the use of affirmations. Affirmations are positive statements that are designed to take you to a more positive and/ or optimistic feeling state. For example, "I am feeling vibrant, energetic, and open to new experiences."

Sometimes, when practicing affirmations, it may feel hard to fully connect to the positive statement. It may even feel as though a part of your body has resistance or tension. When that happens, it likely indicates there is an energetic blockage. A blockage is a subconscious belief that is interfering with your ability to connect to the intention. For example, a blockage for the affirmation of *I am in a vibrant loving relationship* could be the subconscious belief of *I am not lovable.*

In addition to the conscious and subconscious portions of your mind, you have a superconscious mind. Whereas the subconscious mind is the layer of consciousness that holds information from earlier experiences in this lifetime and past lifetimes, the superconscious mind is the layer of consciousness that holds the information about your higher self, your spirit, and the spiritual realm. The model developed by Peter Smith in *Quantum Consciousness: Journey through Other Realms* expands on the concept of the superconscious mind to describe multiple layers of quantum consciousness.

When I receive inquiries about hypnosis, the most common fear I hear is this: "What if I cannot be hypnotized?" So I would like to address that concern. In order to successfully drop into a trance state, to deeper levels of relaxation, and expanded states of consciousness, your conscious mind must be willing to take the back seat. This can take some practice because the conscious mind is used to being in charge and running the show. Remember, the conscious mind is the part of you that has focused on keeping you safe your whole life. When you do hypnosis, you are asking your conscious mind to go off guard, so to speak. Given this, when you choose a hypnotherapist, it is very important that the fit feels good intuitively. While this is true for traditional counseling as well, it is especially true for hypnosis.

When someone contacts me for hypnosis, I will encourage them to check in with their intuition, while we are talking. We often refer to this as a "gut feeling." Your body will tell you whether the facilitator-client relationship is a good fit and whether the timing is good.

In very rare instances, I have had clients who did not go into trance. Usually, it was because they were trying too hard and had put too much pressure on themselves to perform versus trusting their guides. Sometimes, they were experiencing too much physical pain to fully relax. One client decided to stop her session early because she felt she had already received all of her answers.

My clients who have had the most success with hypnosis are the ones who have already been doing some sort of meditation;

are open, curious, and imaginative; and believe that they are worthy of the support.

If you are considering hypnosis, it can be very helpful to prepare by doing guided meditations that activate your creative, imaginative mind in training the conscious mind to relax. There are many types of guided meditations available on YouTube and on various apps, such as Calm and Insight Timer.

I have recorded guided meditations and provide them on my website: kathykwiatkowski.com. When someone contacts me for hypnosis, I will recommend that they listen to these guided meditations. This can help them to acclimate to my voice and it facilitates an easier transition into trance.

Past Life Regression

Information about the past lives you have lived is stored in your subconscious mind. A past life regression (PLR) enables you to access information in your subconscious mind about the previous lives you have lived, including trauma you experienced in those past lives.

Reasons for Doing PLR Hypnotherapy

There are numerous reasons why people choose to do PLR hypnotherapy, including these:

- to learn whether the challenges in your current life are connected to a past life (which is especially helpful for addictions),
- to undo karmic ties with problematic people in your current life,
- to learn more about your experiences in past lives,

- to get information about unexplained physical problems and unexplained phobias in your current life,
- to learn about spiritual gifts and/or spiritual experiences you have had in past lives,
- to identify problematic beliefs connected to past lives that are still active in your current life,
- to confirm information you have received through visions or from other sources,
- and more.

In Diane Morrin's book, *Untying the Karmic Knot*, she describes numerous case studies in which PLR resulted in a change in relationship problems in current time, as well as relief from depression, pain, and other conditions. I have had the same results in my PLR work with clients. Following are two examples from my clinical work.

Past Life Regression Case Study #1, with Sally

Sally, a thirty-nine-year-old woman, came to see me to do a past life regression (PLR) to address what she called, "debilitating anxiety and depression." She reported having suicidal ideation in her teens and had a history of self-injury by means of cutting herself with a blade. She reported feeling "so broken right now." She described her parents as "extremely supportive."

Sally reported that she had been adopted at the age of five. Her history included having a biological father who had been verbally abusive to her biological mother and had substance abuse issues. She reported having one biological sibling who had died from substance abuse. She reported that she had stopped all alcohol use eight years prior to our session, but she still used tobacco and marijuana daily. She felt shame about her tobacco and marijuana use.

Sally had a child-like energy to her. She clearly felt embarrassed about the life challenges she had been having.

Sally had no previous experience with hypnosis. She had several reasons for pursuing a PLR. She had been pushed out of her previous job when her employer eliminated her position and she wanted to understand why that job experience had happened to her. She also wanted healing from the pain she was feeling from that dismissal. She wanted relief from her symptoms of anxiety and depression, and needed to know what direction to go professionally and vocationally.

Following is a brief description of Sally's PLR experience. When Sally first entered her past life, she felt herself on a train and saw herself as a barefoot, teenage boy with dark hair and pale skin, wearing shorts. She felt as though she was either on an adventure or had run away. She had no belongings with her.

To get more information regarding what had led up to this point in time in Sally's past life as the teenage boy on the train, I took Sally back in time, to an earlier time in that life. However, instead of going back in time in that lifetime, Sally moved to a different lifetime in which she was a six- or seven-year-old little girl with pigtails, wearing a white dress and living in Holland. She was playing with other kids in a tulip garden. She felt happy. As the scene progressed, she went to explore a creek. At the creek was a man she did not know. She sensed that she hurt her foot and hit her head. She then saw blood all over her pretty white dress and had the awareness that she had died.

As she moved completely into her spirit and sensed herself looking down at her body, she had access to more information regarding that lifetime. She had an overwhelming feeling of being comforted and at peace. She also had the realization (in the form of a knowing—claircognizance) that the circumstances of her death were to protect her from living through the experience of being harmed by the stranger at the creek.

Sally's experience of seeing her lifetime as a teenage boy on the train reconnected her with her desire to explore and try new things. She reported feeling encouraged and freed up to move forward with her heart's desires. Sally also reported that she had a deep feeling that her current lifetime might be the first time she had "made it into adulthood." To her that explained many of the struggles she had been having with being an adult and it gave her a sense of relief.

In a follow-up email, Sally said the following:

> I was feeling so lost and disoriented in life and somehow seeing and feeling those moments during my PLR gave me better insight into where I needed to be going now. As well as giving me the courage to pursue a direction that has been silently calling to me for so long. Also, the feeling that my soul has potentially never lived to adulthood in my previous lives has explained SO MUCH about why I tend to behave and feel the way I do…. Even after my sessions I continue to connect what I experienced in the PLR session with my current life and it helps me understand myself in a more accepting way.

Past Life Regression Case Study #2, with Judy

Judy, a sixty-one-year-old woman, had no previous experience with PLR. However, she had been practicing and teaching mindfulness for years. She came to see me for a PLR to address difficulties in her relationship with her mother. She described her mother as angrily demanding and overly dependent. Judy felt that these challenges were inhibiting her mother's growth, as well as creating anger and resentment for Judy. Judy had the feeling that somehow their roles were reversed, with Judy feeling more like the mother in their relationship.

In her PLR, Judy accessed a past life during which she lived in a tribe with indigenous people, on land that she described as fertile and forested. Judy saw herself as a forty-year-old male, wearing clothing made of leather and bone. She reported, "I am the leader of the tribe." She experienced a strong connection to the land, which filled her with energy. She reported that in that lifetime, as the tribal leader, she would travel to a small cabin, a day's journey away, to help a young mother with small children. The husband of this young mother had been killed by the tribe and, as the tribal leader, Judy in that past life felt responsible for the wrongdoing.

Over time, the young mother became part of the tribe, ultimately marrying another member of the tribe. Judy recognized this young mother as her own mother in her current life.

Judy's experience of seeing herself caring for and protecting her mother in this past life was transformative. Judy witnessed her mother's strength and resolve in the past life, as the young mother discovered new meaning and connection after the death of her husband. This demonstrated to Judy the strengths that her mother held in her soul lineage.

Judy also felt more empathy for her mother, both in the past life and in her current life.

In a follow-up communication I had with Judy she reported the following.

> *I have been able to establish respectful and strong boundaries with my mother without the feelings of guilt and obligation that I have felt for so long. Over time, she has accepted these boundaries, and she has connected to a larger community and is making changes in her life. We did not work this out through discussion. These changes rest on a shift in understanding that I could act on with clarity. Things are so much better now.... I feel a more sacred connection to the Earth. I can feel that the Earth is alive in me and when I walk through the forests, I feel the landscape alive beneath my feet and how I belong to the land and to the waters. It's almost like I inhabit the way of life I had in my past life. I go to quiet and beautiful natural places—much like those I saw in my past life regression—to connect to the sacred and to find inner peace and wisdom. When I am troubled, the natural environment is always there for me.*

My impression is that, through her PLR, Judy not only reconnected to a past life, but also to the great Divine Creator and Source.

Chapter 6

Life Between Lives Regression

*O*nce you do a past life regression (PLR), which enables you
to drop into the subconscious mind to access information
about all of your experiences in this life and past lives, you can
then expand into the superconscious mind and the greater
layers of the field of quantum consciousness and your spirit.

As I stated at the end of chapter 3, Life Between Lives
(LBL) hypnotherapy was developed by Michael Newton, a psy-
chologist. Certification to practice LBL hypnotherapy is done
through the Michael Newton Institute. The training is based
on over thirty years of research and study, much of it being
summarized in Newton's books, *Journey of Souls* and *Destiny of
Souls*. In Michael Newton's book *Journey of Souls*, he describes
in detail how he did his research and how the LBL hypnotherapy process was developed. You can also learn more about LBL
hypnotherapy on NewtonInstitute.org. Countless case studies
of LBL regressions are available in his books and in the Newton
Institute materials.

I am a Michael Newton Institute-certified LBL facilitator. Through my training and work facilitating LBL sessions, I have learned that often, for the purpose of growth, souls have a very specific plan for experiencing a difficulty or challenge during their incarnation. Those who seek out an LBL session have usually been dealing with some kind of challenge for a while.

An LBL session is a hypnosis session that enables the client to experience being fully in their spirit and in the spiritual realm. How does this work? A typical LBL involves a regression to a past life, going to the end of the past life, dying in the past life, and then crossing over into the spiritual realm. The experience of seeing oneself die is painless, because it is happening in a past life.

In my LBL hypnotherapy work, I get the privilege, regularly, of accompanying my clients to the realm of the nonphysical, to the spiritual realm. The spiritual realm is a beautiful expansive realm of love and light and vibration. Everyone's experience of the spiritual realm is unique to that individual. For that reason, no two LBLs are the same. LBL hypnotherapy gives a person the opportunity to feel their connection to their divine supports (which some think of as their angels or guides) and their connection to All That Is. It is a profound experience.

Reasons for Doing LBL Hypnotherapy

There are countless reasons why a person might choose to do LBL hypnotherapy, including (but not limited to) these:

- to experience being in your soul state,
- to experience connecting with guides and other spiritual beings,

- to have the first-hand experience of your divine support network,
- to learn who is in your soul group,
- to better understand the lessons that you are working on in this life,
- to learn more about your past lives,
- to see if you are on track with your plan for this lifetime,
- to learn more about your spiritual gifts,
- to better understand current life experiences that are related to karma,
- to connect with departed loved ones,
- to receive healing in the spiritual realm,
- to get information about unexplained physical problems and unexplained phobias in your current life,
- to get guidance on how to deal with challenges in your current life,
- and more.

For many people, the most profound aspect of an LBL session is the felt experience of being fully in their spirit and experiencing their divine support. An LBL regression session often includes receiving healing either directly from spiritual beings (angels and guides) or through some other healing experience (such as vibration or healing energy). In an LBL session, the wisdom and information are received and experienced directly by the client rather than through the facilitator. The person being regressed is the receiver of the knowledge.

I would like to share a couple of case studies from my LBL work, as a way of helping you to understand the profound impact of the LBL experience. While every client's experience is unique to them, there are some that are more unusual than others. I have chosen to share one atypical case and one typical case.

Atypical Life Between Lives Regression Case #1, with Jeff

Jeff was sixty-one at the time he contacted me for his LBL regression. He stated he was currently not working because of health issues, but had worked for years as a mechanic. His reason for pursuing an LBL session was because he was "feeling lost and off my path." He was looking for a sense of purpose and some vision of a future.

More than anything, Jeff was in search of healing for multiple physical conditions, including a head injury that had occurred five years earlier. Jeff reported that for a very long time he had felt unable to relax. He disclosed a childhood history of years of being beaten and tormented by a sibling. Jeff told me about painful experiences of betrayal in previous relationships, including in both his marriages. He also was seeking answers to why he had been saved from dying on four occasions of near-death experiences.

When I first meet with someone for an LBL, I always ask about any intuitive gifts or notable spiritual experiences. Jeff reported having had a spiritual experience two months before, during which he saw a white-haired, bearded man wearing a white suit. He also described having the gift of claircognizance, which is the intuitive gift of psychic knowledge. People with claircognizance will say, "I just know things and I don't know how I know them."

Jeff shared with me that he had found feeling vibrations, using singing bowls, and chanting to be helpful and relaxing. He also had a successful practice of using meditation and focusing on the breath to relax.

Everything about Jeff's demeanor was kind and loving. I felt such empathy for the pain he had experienced growing up and the challenges he had experienced throughout his life. I also was amazed at how, despite all his challenges, he felt "the need to help or heal others." He also wondered why he felt that need. He wondered where the knowledge (the intuitive knowing) came from. He wondered who the white-haired, bearded man was. He wondered if he would ever have a truly loving relationship. He wanted to know how to make the most of his gift and, in his words, the answer to a constant question: "What can I do to be a better person?"

Most people who seek an LBL regression session want to know if they are "on my path" and if not, how to course correct. They want to know if they are going in the right direction and if they are fulfilling their purpose. Often, they want to learn more about what their purpose was for coming to planet Earth. Jeff had many of those questions. My intuition told me that the primary purpose for him working with me at this time would be for healing: physical, emotional, and mental healing. Healing was exactly what turned out to be the primary focus of his session.

I am calling Jeff's regression atypical, because it did not follow the usual direction that can happen in an LBL regression and because, as it unfolded, it became clear that a hybrid sort of approach would be needed. Jeff had significant difficulty relaxing throughout his session. He had been unable to relax the day before, when we attempted to do a past life regression, but he still wanted to do the LBL regression. I knew from what had happened the first day that some extra vibration and energy work would be helpful. Throughout Jeff's LBL session, from beginning to end, I used the vibration of a singing bowl to help him relax. As the session progressed, the chiming of the bowl actually opened up his ability to see images and get information.

Once Jeff became accustomed to how information was coming through, he was better able to trust what was happening. Because of his brain injury, he struggled with how to put the images and information into words. He had the sense that he was being shown a lot, but he could not interpret everything. I assured him that all of the information was being translated vibrationally into his subconscious and his energy field, and because of that it would still benefit him.

Following are some more details of his experience. Jeff would experience a cold sensation when entities were present, and he could discern their location and activity by those sensations. There were three entities that would come and go, entering from his left and his right. At one point he felt one of them sitting in his lap. Jeff saw his white-haired, bearded man in much more detail and came to know, beyond any doubt, "This is who is watching over me." The image of this man was the most vivid image he was able to interpret.

He also learned more about changes to make in his current approach to intimacy with women. He was shown a woman with her skirt coming up while salsa dancing, which activated sexual desire in him. He came to understand that this was guidance about how he is approaching relationships. He was being told to stop doing "friends with benefits" in order to have the loving relationship that he was really wanting. He realized that his current approach with women was a way of just going through the motions; instead, he talked about wanting a meaningful attachment.

He saw images of mountains and understood this to mean that where he currently lives is where he is meant to be. This man, who for years had not experienced free thought because of his brain injury, was able to describe images and sensations; after his session, he immediately started freely talking about the experience. Some of his first statements after he returned was "I'm making everyone else happy; I need to focus on my own happiness."

I supported Jeff throughout his LBL session with a variety of energy techniques. Shortly after completing his regression, he said, "My heart feels like it's having to work less hard to beat." During the session I had done a full chakra balancing, the highlight of which was opening his heart chakra. Throughout his session he experienced all the colors of the chakras in a variety of ways. I cleared out stuck energies and enlivened his entire energy body. I also used reiki, which is described later in chapter 9. At the end of the session, I spent some time explaining how hypervigilance impacts the nervous system and I told him that his body now had received the message that it is safe to relax. I suggested that he continue to do heart chakra meditations.

As Jeff left that day, his body language was more fluid and relaxed, and his step was lighter.

The following is an excerpt of an email I received from Jeff the next day.

Good morning, Kathy. I would like to thank you for the experience, so many things have changed inside.

The drive home was the most relaxed I have ever been. All the pounding and pressure of my heart are gone and the peace I feel is almost overwhelming; for the first time, I feel at peace. On so many levels, I thank you for making this happen; my heart has never felt so comfortable. Now with my heart at peace, I feel comfortable with what I have always been doing.

Jeff's guides wanted him to have peace, and with that came the reassurance that he was exactly where he was meant to be.

Life Between Lives Regression Case #2, with Susan

Susan was fifty-seven at the time I met with her to facilitate her LBL regression. She had been considering doing an LBL regression for the previous six months. At the time of our meeting, she was employed full-time in the medical field. Her primary reasons for pursuing an LBL regression had to do with feeling unfulfilled and having low energy. She reported having a deep longing to feel special and loved and she wanted to explore the root of that feeling.

She had multiple questions about her purpose including these: "What am I supposed to be doing to fulfill my soul contract? And, what would help me to better align with my calling and my soul?" She wanted information about the next best step to help with her soul progression. She wanted to know the lessons she was supposed to be working on. She wanted information about her soul mate and who she was meant to be helping and supporting. She also had relationship questions about her current marriage, a past marriage to an abusive spouse, and her current daughter-in-law.

Susan's childhood history included being adopted. After discussing the information that can possibly be obtained regarding adoption, Susan decided she would like to explore these questions: "Was that a contract between me and my birth mother? And, who made that plan?" She did not report any concerns she wanted to explore with regard to her family of origin. Susan struck me as a down-to-earth, caring person with a logical approach to life.

When I asked Susan about any intuitive gifts or notable spiritual experiences she might have, she told me she had the gift of clairaudience. She described times when she would "get a message" that was meant to be shared with someone sitting close to her. She also reported being ostracized by her church group because of this ability. It was clear to me that, when she heard these messages, her only option was to share the information, even if sharing it had negative consequences for her. That told me a lot about her character.

Susan also shared that she had experienced hearing the names of two of her guides (Anya and Micah) while doing a meditation and had sensed herself "pulling back" from connecting beyond the physical realm. Finally, Susan reported having the gift of glossolalia. This is a phenomenon in which an individual speaks in a language or uses speech-like sounds that are unknown to the speaker; this is commonly referred to as "speaking in tongues." She told me that when it would happen it felt calming, "like a soul conversation." We decided to try to get more information about this gift in her LBL regression.

Susan had no previous history of doing hypnosis, except for the past life regression (PLR) session she had done with me the day before. As we were preparing to do her PLR she had reported feeling nervous that she would not be able to go into trance. When doing her PLR, she easily and readily moved into seeing herself in another lifetime.

For her LBL regression, she was eager, open, and trusting of the process. The doubt that had been present prior to her PLR session was now gone.

An LBL regression can include taking the person back in time in their current life to their mother's womb. Because of Susan's history, I felt that going to the womb could be especially beneficial for her. When Susan arrived back in her mother's womb, she was able to have the profound experience of her birth mother's excitement and love for her. Once this was complete, I facilitated Susan's journey to her most recent past life.

The following are a few details of the life she saw. She dropped into her past life at the age of seven and saw herself as a Caucasian girl in Ireland, wearing a shabby cotton dress, waiting outside her cottage for her father. Her name in that life was Sarah. Sarah's mother had died and Sarah lived on a farm with her father and no siblings. I then took Sarah forward in time. She next saw herself getting married in the village, dancing and celebrating with family and friends. When we went forward in time again, she saw herself at the age of seventy-three, lying in bed and near the time of her death. We paused here to get information about people in Sarah's life who were also in Susan's current life. (This is often helpful in resolving relationship issues in one's current life.) Susan learned that her current husband was also her husband in her lifetime as Sarah. Sarah's husband (his name in that past life was Jacob) was at her bedside as she was dying; he was stroking her hair. Susan was moved to tears as she described the scene and realized that her previous life was one of contentment, happiness, and fulfillment. From there, I guided Sarah to the end of that life and facilitated her crossing over into the spiritual realm.

Once a client has died in their past life, they are in the energy of their spirit. During this time, I hold the knowing that any answers and information coming from the client who is sitting in the chair in front of me are actually coming from their spirit. Once the client is able to tell me their spirit name, I address the client by that name.

Susan reported to me that her spirit name is Ashwa, and her spirit color is light blue (indicative of a more advanced soul—according to Michael Newton's research). As Ashwa moved into the spiritual realm, she was greeted by her soul group and her guide Anya. As they reunited, Ashwa sensed their excitement about her return. Then Ashwa told me, "They are sending me energy … but I cannot go to them yet … I have to do something else first."

Ashwa was then taken by her guide to meet with a group of elders. (The elders are wiser beings more advanced than our teacher guides—according to Michael Newton's research.) This was a happy reunion in which Ashwa felt embraced in warmth and praised for doing a good job in her life as Sarah. Ashwa reported, "They are happy … like I overcame something."

We explored more details about Ashwa's elders. Ashwa reported that the names of her elders are Beos, Rasha, Maure, and Tempre, and she said, "They want me to join them."

At this point in the regression, Ashwa started talking in a language I did not know. For the remainder of the regression, she went back and forth between English and the other language. Ashwa informed us (Susan and me) that the other language is the language that she speaks with the elders and that Susan is not meant to be able to interpret the language. Ashwa told us that when the language comes through to Susan, it is meant to direct her. I asked, "How is she doing with following the direction?" And I was told, "Susan is rebellious but she is getting better."

We learned that the elders were preparing Ashwa to also be an elder, and that Ashwa and this group of elders have worked together for a long time. Micah, another one of Susan's guides, was also present at this gathering as a mentor and teacher.

Once a soul is back with their council of elders, it is an opportunity to ask questions on behalf of the client. I believe it is especially important to find out if there is critical information about where the client currently is on their path. In preparation for this, the day before the client's LBL regression, we carefully review and prioritize their questions. The questions are asked through the higher self (through Ashwa for Susan) to the elders, on behalf of the client. In some cases, the client's spirit, their higher self, will answer the questions as well. In Susan's case, she was initially given messages from the elders. Then, the elders left and Ashwa answered the remaining questions.

The following is a summary of what Susan learned from the elders and Ashwa. The first message that was given to Susan from the elders was "be ready." When I tried to get more information about this statement they would not say more. Next, they assured Susan, "You are not alone."

When we moved to asking the questions on Susan's list, Ashwa said, "They don't want her to know … but she can ask." So I proceeded with Susan's questions. Susan was then told that, with regard to her longing to feel loved, that "love was taken away when she was young and this has been a repeated pattern across lifetimes. However, she has broken the pattern now by getting stronger, wiser, and trusting herself." She was told that she would need to "surrender into the knowing that you are not alone," in order to fully release the longing to feel loved. With regard to her purpose, calling, and soul contract, she was told to open and be aware of opportunities to act with love. She was reassured by Ashwa's words, "You have my wisdom." She was also told that she was "close to completing her soul progression ... close to being ready to be with the elders."

With regard to being adopted she was told that it was part of the plan and was for Susan's growth. Susan was meant to face longing and loneliness.

I then asked, "Is there anything more regarding what Susan is meant to be working on?" And received the message, "Be sensitive to the signs, be in tune with the signs, trust."

Some time was then spent exploring questions regarding Susan's daughter-in-law and Susan's desire to help her. Susan was shown a past life that she had shared with her current daughter-in-law during which they were sisters. In that lifetime, Susan left her sister behind, but not by choice.

With regard to Susan's question about helping others, she was told, "She will help many ... trust your heart ... it will be good."

With regard to her low energy, she was told that she would soon go home and to not worry. With regard to her karma with her abusive ex-husband and whether it was part of her plan for this journey, she was told, "They have been together in many different lives ... with the same pattern ... this time she is set free." She was also told that he is not a soul mate.

At the conclusion of this period of asking questions, I asked Ashwa, "Are there any other experiences in the spiritual realm that would be important for Susan to have today?" I was told, "No ... the experience is complete for today."

I asked, "Is there any other information that would be important for Susan to have?" The answer was again no. I like to ask these two questions to be sure that the client gets the most out of their experience in the spiritual realm. We ended the session by thanking Ashwa for all her support and assistance, and then returned to present consciousness.

I have had the opportunity to exchange emails with Susan since her session. Here are a few statements, in her words, about what has happened since her LBL regression.

> *I have such a lightness about me since I got back from Idaho. I can honestly say that I have a level of peace that I have never known. I feel like I have given myself permission to explore and utilize the gifts that I shut down long ago.... I feel my spirit guides with me more now.... I am excited about whatever lies ahead ... Ashwa has spoken to me in the form of internal dialogue ... I get a warm feeling in my chest and then I feel her presence ... her influence must come through because I am amazed at the insight that I am given ... I had a lady at a bookstore ask me out of the blue if I did readings ... friends and family have commented on how different I am ... I feel closure about my abusive ex-husband ... I feel set free ... I feel that I have unblocked a channel that has allowed more wisdom and understanding to flow ... I feel like I am getting closer to my soul self and I like her!*

Once a person has an LBL regression experience, any beliefs about being abandoned, unloved, unlovable, faulty, or unimportant are shifted at a very deep level. Because an

LBL session takes someone to their superconscious mind, it is impossible to describe the results in a linear way. An LBL journey impacts a person's energetic body, emotional body, and mental body.

My greatest joy is learning from my clients about the profound impact of their LBL session, even months later.

My journey beyond traditional counseling has not stopped with my LBL regression and PLR work. When I reflect on my initial decision to extend my work to include LBL regressions and PLRs, I can see how that was just the beginning of following my spiritual path and my purpose in this lifetime. I can see now that it was the gateway to a whole new level of helping people to see themselves in truth and to stand in their brilliance.

Much to my surprise, I then found myself feeling that there was something even more to do. That something was learning how to facilitate healing from the more expanded realms of consciousness through the Quantum Consciousness Experience (QCE) and other quantum journeys. Choosing to expand my work these days has felt like a natural evolution of my work and my soul purpose.

Chapter 7

Quantum Healing Using QCE and Quantum Journeys

Expanding My Work

*O*ne of my intentions for what I am offering in this book is to help you understand the potential benefits of a holistic approach to your healing journey. My focus in this chapter is to provide details about the experience of quantum healing approaches more so than to explain quantum science theories. As such, quantum healing approaches offer many ideas, perspectives, and theories that can be used to profoundly expand and accelerate the healing process. In fact, quantum "healing" isn't really about healing, because quantum works from the premise that there is actually nothing to heal. Personally, I love that! As a therapist, though, I have to say that the work creates a major shift in perspective on the physical level.

In quantum work, the objective, the goal, is for the client to simply remember themself in truth by accessing their true authentic self, their spirit. This then shifts what is happening in the client's current experience.

How does this happen?

Quantum science purports that each of us is a limitless expansive being whose consciousness exists in multiple dimensions all at the same time and each of us holds all of the universe within us. In the quantum field there is no linear time: no past and no future. Everything exists in now time. What we have thought of as "past lives" are actually occurring simultaneously with our current life experience. Also, the future realities of your current life experience are happening now.

With quantum healing, you have access to your expanded states of consciousness and the deep wisdom of the universe that flows through all things. With regard to healing physical, emotional, and spiritual difficulties in your current life, the implications of this are immense. When we are in the middle of a human struggle, we often hang on to the hope of *It will get better in time,* and then it does. You actually have the power within you to bring that future reality into your now experience. Change does not have to take time. In the quantum field, time does not exist. This "truth" was also reported by the clients that Michael Newton regressed during his research.

Quantum healing techniques are based on several principles of quantum science, including the observer effect, non-locality, entanglement, and holograms. Initially the idea of learning about quantum science intimidated me. However, learning just a few basic principles proved to be easy and very helpful. In his book, *Quantum Consciousness: Journey through Other Realms,* Peter Smith describes in detail how he expanded on the ideas of quantum physics to develop his Quantum Consciousness

Experience (QCE). The QCE and the other quantum journeys described in this chapter involve a guided process for moving out beyond the human energy field into the more expanded energy fields and realms of your higher self, your spirit, the spiritual realms, and the expanding levels of consciousness in the quantum field.

This process is similar to a guided meditation, but much more impactful. In this high vibrational state, there is a sense of freedom and ease. The healing and/or wisdom exchanged is sent holographically out through all your lives and dimensions forever, thereby raising the vibrational frequency of all your selves.

The two teachers from whom I have learned quantum healing techniques are Dr. Sue Morter and Peter Smith. In this chapter, I would like to describe Peter Smith's work and the opportunities for healing that are available with the quantum journeys he has developed.

But before doing so, let me tell you a little story about how I came to expand my work into doing quantum healing. Years ago, when I attended my LBL training with the Michael Newton Institute (MNI), I heard several facilitators from MNI speaking very highly of someone named Peter Smith. I was unaware of him at the time. The way that others were speaking of him made me feel like I wanted to meet him and study with him. After a few years of settling into my LBL work, I started researching Peter's work. Peter Smith is a clinical hypnotherapist who worked closely with Michael Newton as a colleague and a friend, and he is the co-founder of the Institute for Quantum Consciousness. He was an LBL hypnotherapist for years and was the president of the Michael Newton Institute from 2009 to 2018.

Since Michael's passing (or more correctly, his transition to the nonphysical realm) in 2016, Peter has taken the LBL work and expanded upon it. Peter's work does not replace the work of Michael Newton and he himself has told me that Michael would say to him, "There's always more."

Peter continues to be closely involved with the MNI in an advisory role and in promoting the legacy of Michael Newton. I knew that Peter was based in Australia, and that he occasionally traveled to California to do trainings. However, I was also willing to travel to Australia if need be. My spirit was calling me to expand my work and I knew intuitively this was the expansion I was meant to do.

Right when I was planning to begin training with Peter, COVID-19 hit, and no one was traveling anywhere. At first this seemed like a major roadblock to my next level of work. However, the impact of the COVID-19 pandemic actually led to the opening of doors for online training. (I believe this is an example of how something can appear like a problem from the human perspective when something even better is being orchestrated by our spirit or our guides.) In the past year I have had the privilege of learning quantum healing techniques directly from Peter and his colleagues through extensive online training.

Quantum Consciousness Experience (QCE)

One of the quantum healing techniques developed by Peter, one that I now offer, is the Quantum Consciousness Experience (QCE). It is designed to take you on a journey into your quantum field, your individual universe, which is also connected to the rest of All That Is in the universe. It is a journey of expansion into the layers of consciousness that hold information about all of your existences across all time and space, including existences in other bodies on other planets.

The QCE provides the opportunity to access wisdom and/ or receive or offer healing from one's existences across multiple dimensions including stored consciousness, alternate consciousness, parallel consciousness, interdimensional consciousness, and eternal consciousness. On the next page is a diagram explaining the Expanding Realms of Consciousness Model developed by Peter Smith.

In the quantum field, we can access alternate realities of ourselves. What does this mean? Every time each of us came to a fork in the road, faced with an important choice, we created a replication of ourself in an alternate reality; a self who made the other choice. For example, when I chose to be a counselor, an alternate reality of me took a different path, making a different choice. There is also an alternate reality of me who chose to marry a different person and another who chose to live in a different place.

In a QCE, the process begins with identifying a high vibrational intention for the journey. This intention-setting process begins to activate your expansion to the greater realms of consciousness. Shifting into different frequencies from an expanded state offers access to information about your existences across time and space. During the QCE, an invitation is offered to your other selves who would like to step forward to offer wisdom, to give healing, or to receive healing. The journey has endless possibilities.

The journey involves exploring these other realms from the realm of your present consciousness, and connecting it all back to the high vibrational intention set for the journey.

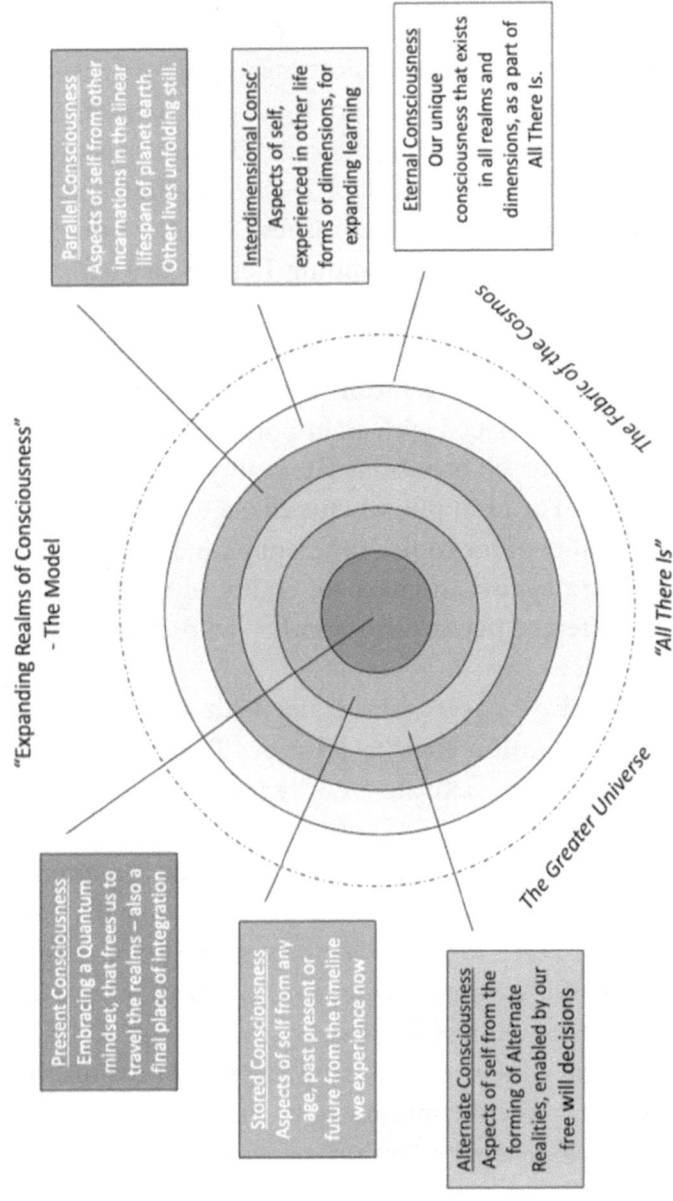

"Expanding Realms of Consciousness"
- The Model

The Fabric of the Cosmos

"All There Is"

The Greater Universe

Parallel Consciousness
Aspects of self from other incarnations in the linear lifespan of planet earth. Other lives unfolding still.

Interdimensional Consc'
Aspects of self, experienced in other life forms or dimensions, for expanding learning

Eternal Consciousness
Our unique consciousness that exists in all realms and dimensions, as a part of All There Is.

Present Consciousness
Embracing a Quantum mindset, that frees us to travel the realms – also a final place of integration

Stored Consciousness
Aspects of self from any age, past present or future from the timeline we experience now

Alternate Consciousness
Aspects of self from the forming of Alternate Realities, enabled by our free will decisions

Much like following an LBL regression, QCE experiences and wisdom are then integrated into a person's present consciousness, to impact the remainder of the journey in this lifetime.

One of the primary differences between an LBL regression and a QCE is the way in which the journey is facilitated. With hypnosis and LBL, you are guided to relax and go down into deeper states of consciousness. With a QCE, you are guided to expand out to other realms of consciousness. Some facilitators, including me, are in the process of blending quantum guidance with LBL regression. As with the LBL and the PLR work, I have done these journeys myself and found them to be helpful beyond anything I could have imagined.

Quantum Journeys

In addition to offering the QCE to clients, I offer other types of powerful quantum journeys, all developed by Peter. These journeys include the following variations:

- the infinity journey,
- the vibrational echoes journey,
- the empath journey,
- the intergenerational journey,
- the powerful parallels journey,
- the multidimensional journey, and
- the cosmic journey.

Following is a brief description of each journey. As with the QCE, these journeys also start with setting a high vibrational intention for the journey. All these journeys offer the opportunity to understand the greater purpose of your current experiences, and to positively impact the collective consciousness through the sharing of wisdom and higher vibrations. As you heal and grow, you naturally have a positive impact throughout the collective consciousness of humanity.

Infinity Journey

This type of quantum journey offers the opportunity to call forward the ancient wisdoms from the lineage of your soul, to absorb the wisdoms available from Gaia (Mother Earth), and to access and absorb universal energies and light vibrations from other civilizations. These wisdoms and energies are shared across the soul lineage, all for the purpose of reminding humanity of our collective magnificence. It is an opportunity to remember that you are a bridge between this planet and the cosmos, and an advocate of light for the greater good of all humanity.

Vibrational Echoes Journey

Any difficulty that you are having in your life is a request for resonance with the vibration of your spirit and All That Is. This journey offers the opportunity to take an expanded states-of-awareness view of current physical or emotional distress, so that you can understand the messages being offered by the current distress. As that unfolds you are then more able to transcend the distress of lower denser energies to achieve resonance with your natural state of love as part of All That Is. You also have the opportunity to learn the greater purpose of your current experience.

Empath Journey

This journey is specifically designed to support the empaths and highly sensitive people of the world. This journey gives you the opportunity to transcend the noise of the world, to feel your deepest authenticity, to explore your gifts and their purpose for yourself and humanity, and to extend this knowing and new vibration throughout your life path. The opportunity is offered to learn how to observe and not absorb, to understand deeply what is yours and what is not, to use your energetic discernment, and to rejoice in your difference. All of this is then shared throughout the collective consciousness for the good of all humanity.

Intergenerational Journey

Difficult energies can be passed down through generations. This type of journey offers the opportunity to understand the greater purpose of incarnating into your family, to interact with both lines of the ancestors for the purpose of clearing energetic inheritance and intergenerational trauma, to set family lines free from anything that is holding them back, and to pass that on to future generations. You also have the opportunity to offer this resonance and healing to the collective consciousness of humanity.

Powerful Parallels Journey

Your other experiences on planet Earth, in other bodies, in other times, have given you many skills and resources. The powerful parallels journey offers the opportunity to access the incredible wisdom and resources of your soul lineage. This is a journey into the realm of parallel consciousness to claim the wisdom, resources, and strengths you already have and to bring those into the here and now to serve you and all of humanity.

Multidimensional Journey

You have access to skills and resources from *other planets and dimensions* through the portal of your human presence. This journey offers the opportunity to explore your multidimensional existence, to access those skills and resources from other existences on other planets in other dimensions, to experience them firsthand, and to bring the remembering of them into your current experience and human state.

Cosmic Journey

This journey offers the opportunity to acquire a deep knowing of who you truly are as a spiritual being, why you chose to come to planet Earth at this time, and to remember what support and resources are available to you. This journey is especially helpful for those who feel out of place here on planet Earth and/or have felt uncomfortable in their bodies for much of their life.

Quantum Journeys Are Individually Impactful

The impact of a quantum journey is as highly individualized as your soul journey. The one outcome across all sessions I have facilitated is the experience of feeling and seeing your magnificence. It is such an incredibly moving and humbling experience to bear witness as a client opens to the whole of who they are and fully realizes their brilliance, their power, and the gifts they are bringing to the world. The experience of transcending your current situation and your human conditioning to gain a broader perspective from the viewpoint of spirit is beyond description. I feel like I cannot say it enough that each and every one of us is here on this planet at this time for a very important reason. Once you return to resonance with the vibration of All That Is, the knowing of this is clear.

The empath journey is especially helpful for those who have felt burdened by their sensitivity. When one client, who did an empath journey, connected with her big, fun, magical energy, she discovered her gift of bringing her magic maker energy to others. This discovery allowed her to release anxiety and rest into a feeling of ease and well-being.

A client who did a vibrational echoes journey transcended the vibration of frustration and was able to see it as "just the human condition." From there he saw himself as an energy with light around him, traveling through time and space. This brought a sense of profound peacefulness.

A client who took the multidimensional journey transcended the vibration of fear and said the following during her more expanded state: "Now I can see the whole pattern ... I can see how important it is for me to open up to receiving love, and how that then enables me to flow a more complete love to others."

For my own intergenerational journey, I set the high vibrational intention of "releasing and relaxing into the flow of abundance, trusting the flow." During the journey I was able to release my maternal ancestors from generations of panic and a sense of desperation. I was then able to help them open and connect with the abundance that flows through all things. In connecting with my paternal ancestors, I was able to set them free from the feeling of loneliness, dutifully carrying the burden of providing for others while not considering their own needs. I also had the lovely and very intimate experience of connecting with the energy of my father who had died thirty years earlier. The culmination of the journey was connecting with the deep knowing of the abundance that I am.

These are just a few examples of the wisdom, healing, and transcendence that are possible with a quantum journey.

Chapter 8

Two Techniques Learned from Dr. Sue Morter

BioEnergetic Synchronization Technique Release

*T*he quantum healing techniques I will share in this chapter are the ones I learned from Dr. Sue Morter. Dr. Sue Morter's father, M. T. Morter Jr., DC (Doctor of Chiropractic), was a pioneer in the field of energy medicine, and he developed the BioEnergetic Synchronization Technique, or B.E.S.T., as it is known. Dr. Sue (as she is known to her students and patients), her father, and her brother took B.E.S.T. and expanded on it by developing a self-administered version called B.E.S.T. Release.

I was fortunate to have the opportunity to learn this technique from Dr. Sue and, in using this technique with clients, I have seen profound responses, including one client's ability to let go of a pattern of worrying about what others were thinking of her, which had been happening for decades. Another client was able to break out of a long-standing pattern of avoidance to start speaking up in an assertive way. B.E.S.T. Release is designed to identify and clear out subconscious beliefs and emotions that interfere with the kind of life a person wants to be living. This clearing out addresses energy blockages or gaps in the third chakra, located in the solar plexus, that have occurred across time and space (see chapter 9). The technique can be self-administered or done with a partner. I believe that initially it is easier to do it with a partner.

Video demonstrations of the Morter March, mPower Step, B.E.S.T. Release, and Muscle Testing can be found on the Morter Institute Website, drsuemorter.com. The Morter March and mPower stance are designed to activate the brain centers in very specific ways. Because of that, they are complex and are most effective when all components of the process are followed.

A summary of the steps follows. The B.E.S.T. Release process starts by identifying a goal or ideal belief. Even though the purpose of the process is to clear out subconscious beliefs and emotions that are interfering, the goal or belief needs to be stated in positive terms.

Some examples are these:

- I am free of pain.
- I am following my heart's desires guilt free.
- I am feeling full of vitality and energy.
- I feel free to speak my mind.
- I deeply trust that I am fully supported.

In essence, you are stating how you want your life to be.

I find that when a client and I set the goal together, the client begins to access the felt sense of relief, even before doing the rest of the process.

Once the belief or goal is identified, muscle testing is used to assess if the belief (i.e., the goal) causes the muscle to go weak.

There are several ways to do muscle testing. When I am working with clients, I use the technique of the arm raised to the side. The goal is first tested with client's eyes open (the process for assessing conscious blocks). If the arm muscle goes weak in response to the stated goal, that goal or belief becomes the belief to focus on for the process. If the muscle tests strong in response to the stated goal, then the goal is tested with eyes closed (the process for assessing subconscious blocks). If the goal tests strong again, there is no need for clearing and the client can focus on a different goal.

Assuming the muscle tested weak either with eyes open or eyes closed, muscle testing is next used to assess the reactive emotion that causes weakness. Six emotions are tested: fear, anger, love, sadness, enjoyment, and judgment. When the muscle tests weak on a particular emotion, it announces that something overwhelming about that emotion is stored in the subconscious.

It may be that several emotions cause the muscle to go weak. In the event of that happening, muscle testing cycles back until the process narrows down to the one emotion that causes the muscle to go the weakest. Once the emotion associated with the belief has been identified, the process of updating the belief starts.

Updating the belief system is done by the client adopting a specific stance (either the Morter March or the more advanced mPower Step), and holding that stance while focusing on the following thought: "I embrace, forgive, and release any interference associated with [insert the emotion associated with the belief] as it relates to my goal, known and unknown, conscious and unconscious, past, present, and future."

The client continues to hold the stance, inhales, holding their breath, exhales, and then switches to the other side. This is repeated at least twice on each side. I often find that clients want to repeat the updating process three times.

I believe that including "past, present, and future" in the statement activates the quantum field and enables the clearing to happen across time and space.

Once the updating process is complete, I muscle test the belief again to see whether it tests strong. If it does not test strong, we explore whether there is another closely related belief to work with or whether to go through the updating process again focusing on another emotion.

When I work with clients and hold the knowing of our quantum entanglement, it adds to the potency of the process.

Dr. Sue's perspective on the separation of subconscious memory from conscious intention matches what I have presented here about how human conditioning creates a closing off from your higher self and a forgetting of the true nature of divine support from the universe.

Central Channel Breath

Dr. Sue also teaches a type of breathing she calls Central Channel Breath (CCB). CCB cycles the energy of the higher self and all that we are energetically connected to in the universe through the physical body.

This type of breathing focuses on imagining that you are breathing in from above the head, down through four anchor points in the central channel (the center of the brain behind the eyes, the center of the throat, the center of the chest, and the base of the spine), and into the earth. While doing CCB, you simultaneously gently contract and lift the pelvic floor.

Once you have done one cycle from above to below, you then do a cycle from below to above by imagining that you are breathing up through the legs into the belly, and exhaling up through the solar plexus, heart, throat, and the head to spirit above.

Quantum and energy healing practices are nurturing for the soul. I continue to use Dr. Sue's Energy Codes on a regular basis and find them to be very effective. Numerous types of breathing practices are incorporated into the Energy Codes. Using the Energy Codes to restore energy flow through the body is a powerful method of opening up to and remembering the truth of who we are. Video demonstrations of the processes that I have described so far can be found on Dr. Sue's website at drsuemorter.com/energycodesbook/, under the tabs for anchoring code and clearing code.

The next chapter offers more understanding of the importance of addressing gaps, imbalances, and blockages in your energy field.

Chapter 9

Energy Medicine and Energy Psychology

A Human Body's Energy Vibrates

*S*cientists have provided convincing evidence that the energy contained in the human body vibrates at a variety of frequencies. As mentioned previously, your body has a human energy field (HEF), and your HEF is made up of vibrating energy particles.

Energy medicine is founded on the principle that disease (dis-ease, meaning "a lack of ease") is the result of disruptions in the human energy field. Your life force energy strengthens the immune system and the body's ability to heal itself. Vibrational energy experts study what creates high and low vibrational frequencies in the body and the effect of vibrational frequencies on the physical body.

A large body of research has examined the effects of meditation, chanting, and deep breathing on the functioning of human cells and the health of the physical body. Additionally, thoughts themselves are energy signals and have a vibrational frequency. Thinking actually burns energy. Your emotions are energy running through your body. In fact, one of the most powerful ways to process emotion is to be mindfully present with the sensations in the body versus being in the story about the emotion.

Your spirit is energy and therefore has a vibrational frequency. When you correct disruptions and imbalances in your energy body—these would have been caused by negative or overwhelming experiences—you open up the flow of energy in and through your body. Acupuncture is specifically designed to open the flow of energy in your body. When there are no blockages or gaps in your energy field, you can more easily access the whole of who you are, your higher self, your spirit. For this reason, it is very important to understand your energy body, especially the chakras and how they influence your symptoms (physically, emotionally, and mentally).

Anodea Judith is a leading authority on the integration of chakras; she holds a PhD in health and human services and an MA in clinical psychology. In her book *Eastern Body, Western Mind: Psychology and the Chakra System As a Path to the Self,* she provides a deep exploration of the chakra system, including how it develops, and its significance with regard to healing. She provides a detailed roadmap for healing energy imbalances and spiritual transformation. Judith states the following.

> *The chakra system is a seven-leveled philosophical model of the universe. Chakras have come to the West through the tradition and practice of yoga ... a discipline designed to yoke together the individual with*

the divine ... A chakra is a center of organization that receives, assimilates and expresses life force energy.

Similarly, in his book *Healing Body, Mind & Spirit*, Howard Batie, an energy-based healing therapist, states the following.

The purpose or function of the human chakra system is to take in higher-dimensional energy from the Universal Energy Field all around us and translate or step down its frequency of vibration to that which can be used within the physical body.

I like to think of this process as the integration of body and spirit. Dr. Sue Morter also talks about this stepping-down process of integrating the higher self with the human self.

Energy medicine and energy psychology offer powerful techniques for correcting disturbances and imbalances in your HEF. As mentioned previously in the discussion about the subconscious mind in chapter 1, your false beliefs about yourself and the world are stored in your subconscious mind. These subconscious beliefs affect your energy body. When you incarnated into your human body, into that little fetus in the womb, your big bright intelligent energy field compacted itself into that physical space. As you experience life, the information associated with your life experiences impacts your energy field. This is why complete healing of your body, mind, and spirit requires addressing blockages, gaps, imbalances, and entanglements in the energy body.

I am presenting several different modalities for energy healing and working with your energy body. The modalities

I will discuss include energy medicine, energy tapping (also referred to as Emotional Freedom Technique or EFT), reiki, qigong, chakra clearing with crystals, and chakra clearing with a pendulum. Because the energy body runs throughout and extends beyond the physical body, each one of these modalities is a way of working with the places where the energy body interfaces with the physical body.

Moving the energy in your body creates physical sensations. The extent to which you feel these sensations depends on your attunement to or your awareness of your body. When energy is moved in the body it also creates a shift in your thoughts. For example, energy work can take you from being in your head with racing thoughts (that would be the gas pedal state of the sympathetic nervous system overdrive discussed previously), to feeling calm and in your body (in your WOT, as described in chapter 2).

I use a combination of reiki and energy clearing to accomplish this for my clients.

You can move the energy in your body yourself and thereby impact your energy body in a positive way without any special training. By doing this, your attitude and perspective on the day can change. For example, if I wake in the morning feeling tired or groggy, once I move the energy in my body, I have thoughts of positive expectation about the day. I feel lighter and more eager to start my day.

When you know how to enliven your energy field and how to calm the nervous system with energy techniques, you realize that you can have so much more control over how you feel, how you respond to your environment, and how much joy you get from life.

Try This Exercise: Enlivening Your Energy Body

You can do this exercise anytime to clear your mind and enliven your body.

Once again, begin by taking a long slow breath, bringing all of your awareness to your physical body. Now, start lightly tapping with the fingertips of both hands on the base of the back of your neck, right where your neck meets your upper back. Tap up the back of your neck and head lightly, to the front of your head; down and across the forehead, temples, jaw, and cheeks. Continue down the sides of your neck to your collar bones.

Once you reach the front of your body, start lightly patting down the top side of one outstretched arm to the back of the hand, then turn the hand over and pat the palm side of the hand and up the underside of the arm to the armpit, and then across the chest to the other arm.

It is important to pat the armpits really well, because energy can get tucked away in those spots.

Once you have gone across the body and up and back on the other arm, pat down your front body, chest, belly, lower belly, and groin area (another very important area where energy can get trapped). Pat inside the legs, down the legs, over the top of each foot, and up the back of the legs. As you come up the back of the legs, once you get to the buttocks, use your fists to lightly pat and massage the buttocks and lower back. Then shake your whole body, bounce, and twist.

Circle your shoulders up and back to really move the energy down your back body with your shoulder blades. Then, finish the process off by massaging your feet, pulling the energy off your toes, lightly slapping the bottom of your feet to open the chakras at the bottom of the feet, and gently shaking each foot as you hold each leg right above the ankle.

Pause and notice how your body feels. This whole process takes only five minutes, and it totally resets your system for the day. I do this first thing every morning.

Once you have tried this technique, journal your answers to the following questions.

- What area of your body benefitted the most from this exercise?
- Was there a part of your body that you avoided patting? Why might that be?
- Did you have the urge to add something more to the exercise?
- When in the process did you start to notice more clarity of mind?

Radiant Circuits

Another amazing resource that you have in your energy body for clearing your mind and shifting your perspective is the radiant circuits. The exercise that you just completed included some aspects of activating the radiant circuits. Radiant circuits in the energy body are directly connected to the feeling of joy. When the radiant circuits are activated, you can experience a lighter inner feeling of appreciation or gratitude, despite whatever is going on around you. These energy circuits do not follow a set pattern and can actually travel to wherever they are needed in the body.

Radiant circuits were first named *strange flows*, because they do not follow a set pattern in the body. They have also been referred to as *psychic circuits*, because of how they respond to one's thoughts. Activating the radiant circuits calms the nervous system, strengthens your energy field, and enhances your natural healing capacity. There are numerous ways to work with and activate the radiant circuits. Activating the radiant circuits can be directed with thought and also by tracing them on the body in a variety of ways. Here are a few simple ways to work with your radiant circuits.

- The next time that you are in the feeling state of happiness, relaxation, and ease, tap on your third eye (the space right between your eyebrows) for about 15 seconds.

- Using the middle finger of both hands, place one middle finger in your belly button and the other middle finger on your third eye. Then, press in and pull up. Hold that for about 30 seconds.

- Using both hands, trace heart symbols along the front of the body. Start with your face, then your chest and torso, then your pelvis, then your whole body. Do this at least three times in each area, but feel free to do it even more times than that.

- Look at something beautiful, such as a sunset or a beautiful piece of art.

- Spend time with someone you love and/or a pet that you cherish.

These are just a few examples of how to activate the radiant circuits.

There are several resources available online that explain the radiant circuits more fully. Donna Eden offers a free class that explains them, and you can also find YouTube videos. I like the videos on YouTube by Prune Harris.

Other Ways to Move Energy

The exercises above are just a few examples of how to start moving the energy in your body.

Because all the information can sometimes be overwhelming, I like to suggest to clients that they start small, with some of the basics. In Donna Eden's book, *The Little Book of Energy Medicine: The Essential Guide to Balancing Your Body's Energies*, you can find detailed exercises for working with your energy field in ways that address a wide range of physical and emotional issues. I like this book because the exercises are simple, easy to learn, and clearly explained.

In Dr. Sue Morter's book, *The Energy Codes: The 7-Step System to Awaken Your Spirit, Heal Your Body, and Live Your Best Life*, you will learn more about your energy systems and how to maximize these systems using specific breathing techniques and body postures. I especially like the way Dr. Morter incorporates yoga philosophy, *asana*, and the chakras into her system of the Energy Codes.

Energy Tapping

Energy tapping is an energy technique that builds on the healing methods of acupuncture. However, instead of using needles, you use two fingers to tap on acupressure points along the meridians—the energy pathways—of the energy body. The tapping stimulates points along these meridians.

Tapping has become more mainstream in the past few years thanks to a system called the Tapping Solution, developed by Nick and Jessica Ortner. The Tapping Solution is available in many formats, including an easy-to-use app on your smartphone.

Another resource is the book *Energy Tapping: How to Rapidly Eliminate Anxiety, Depression, Cravings, and More Using Energy Psychology*, written by Fred P. Gallo, PhD, and Harry Vincenzi, EdD.

The process of energy tapping involves the following steps:

1. think about the issue that is troubling you most or think about your current symptom,

2. rate the level of severity of discomfort from zero to ten, where ten is the most severe,

3. follow a series of tapping specific acupressure points while making certain statements, and

4. rate the level of severity again.

Some protocols also involve rolling the eyes and humming. You repeat the protocols until the level of severity or distress is at zero or one. As you repeat this process, you will notice that your thoughts about the issue or problem begin to change. The process also gives you the opportunity to be present with what you are feeling while relaxing your nervous system.

If you use the Tapping Solution app, you are given some guidance and coaching on locating the issue in your body, gradually releasing the current feelings of distress, and connecting with positive cognitions and positive felt states. When you connect with the more positive thoughts and positive feelings in your body, your nervous system calms down.

Tapping is a powerful way to regulate your nervous system by creating a clear flow of energy throughout your energy bodies.

Reiki

Reiki is described as spiritually guided life force energy. All energy healing or energy medicine uses life force energy (that Universal Energy Field that Howard Batie refers to), but it is believed that not all energy healers use reiki. I was taught that reiki is a special kind of healing energy that can only be channeled once you have received an attunement from a reiki master. It is believed by some that during the attunement, adjustments are made in one's chakras and energy body as well as one's consciousness in order to channel the reiki energy. The attunement is a form of linking up to the source of reiki energy, and it has the potential to increase one's access to their intuitive gifts.

The reiki master I worked with provided three levels of attunement to become a reiki master. After my first attunement experience, I was able to easily access and apply reiki energy. Each attunement enhances the channeling of the energy. While I did the attunements for the purpose of being able to offer the healing to others, I also found the attunements to be healing for me.

Once reiki energy has been received, one can access it for the remainder of one's life and use reiki for healing of self and others. Providing reiki to another does NOT involve contact with the body. Rather, the reiki practitioner holds their hands above the body, at varying distances, depending on how the reiki energy is coming through for the client's needs.

I learned Usui Reiki, which is the Western version of the reiki originating in Japan; Dr. Mikao Usui was the founder of reiki. Other reiki styles have developed, many of which are variations of the reiki founded by Dr. Usui.

Qigong

In March 2020, the whole world shut down due to the COVID-19 pandemic. I moved my clinical practice from in-person to online remote sessions. For months, I worked from home, seeing the same number of clients I would normally see in my office. I learned that all the trauma therapies and the hypnotherapy I was doing were equally powerful when done remotely. I also learned that energy work can be just as effective across the country as across the room.

For a couple of years before the pandemic shutdown, I had known of and experienced energy healing. I had been trained in reiki and had been using that for myself and others. I had been doing tapping (although not consistently) and had been receiving energy-based massage and other energy-based treatments. But energy practices were not yet a part of my daily life.

My inconsistent practice of energy medicine changed in March 2020, and I now have a local energy medicine practitioner, University of Idaho professor, Alan Nasypany, EdD, of Resource Energetics, to thank for that. Dr. Nasypany decided to offer an online class to teach qigong and some other energy healing techniques. Because I was working from home,

I was able to participate in the class from the comfort of my own living room. Several times a week we met and did the qigong practices developed by Robert Peng and taught by Dr. Nasypany. I also learned and practiced other energy medicine techniques developed by Dr. Nasypany (some of which are available through his website at resourceenergetics.com). That class launched me into what today is a daily qigong practice. I have also integrated many of his techniques for clearing energy and moving energy into my daily self-care as well as my work with clients.

Qigong practices enable us to connect with and experience the power of our life force energy, our spirit. There are active and passive qigong practices. Both types involve using mental focusing, slow, deep, smooth breathing, and an awareness or sensing into the qi energy (*qi* is pronounced *chee*; it is your energy field and the energy of the universe). For some people, sensing the qi occurs naturally. For some, it may take practice to sense this energy. And for others, the energy cannot be sensed at all, but rather only imagined. The qi is present even if you do not sense it.

The active form of qigong involves slow movement of the body while breathing deeply and sensing the qi. The passive form involves mental focus, breathing, and sensing, without movement or with static postures. The National Center for Complementary and Integrative Health describes qigong as follows.

> *Qigong, pronounced "chi gong," was developed in China thousands of years ago as part of traditional Chinese medicine. It involves using exercises to optimize energy within the body, mind, and spirit,*

with the goal of improving and maintaining health and well-being. Qigong has both psychological and physical components and involves the regulation of the mind, breath, and body's movement and posture. In most forms of qigong: Breath is slow, long, and deep. Breath patterns may switch from abdominal breathing to breathing combined with speech sounds. Movements are typically gentle and smooth, aimed for relaxation. Mind regulation includes focusing one's attention and visualization.

Even though I am just at the beginning of learning these practices, I am already experiencing their power. I find some of them to be enlivening and others to be calming and settling. I especially like the way in which I can expand out into my energy field and then feel the energy of the universe moving through me.

The only prerequisite for practicing qigong is the ability to smile. Begin by smiling and then widen the space between your eyes (also smiling). Engaging your journey this way is practicing qigong. It will transform your entire life. It changes the lens from which you perceive the world, and it rewires your nervous system by sending signs of safety and love.

The effect of qigong on physical health is being studied. Many of the published studies show promise with regard to a decrease in the symptoms studied and an improvement in overall quality of life. However, as often happens with scientific studies, many of the studies also report the need for further research.

The resource that I currently use for qigong is *The Master Key: Qigong Secrets for Vitality, Love and Wisdom* by Robert

Peng. There are also numerous learning opportunities available through his website at robertpeng.com.

Chakra Clearing

In *The Little Book of Energy Medicine*, Donna Eden states that the chakras "are believed to energetically record every emotionally significant event you experience." Chakra clearing can be accomplished in many ways: by using Donna Eden's energy medicine techniques, Dr. Sue Morter's Energy Codes, reiki, chanting, crystal singing bowls, or crystals and a pendulum. Each chakra has a corresponding color and specific crystals associated with them. Each chakra also has a specific vibrational frequency; and there are specific sounds that correspond to each. I have summarized that information in the seven charts below. The frequency associated with chanting the sound for the chakra is believed to both clear and stabilize the chakra.

First Chakra: Root Chakra

location	coccyx, base of the spine
color	red
function	vitality, life force, survival, instincts, material world, security
underactive	lack of stamina, poor focus, disorganized, financial problems, fearful, anxious
overactive	overeating, greed, hoarding

physical manifestation	poor circulation, varicose veins, swollen feet or legs, lower back pain
gems and crystals	garnet, hematite, red jasper, ruby, black tourmaline, obsidian
sound vibration	lam

Second Chakra: Sacral Chakra

location	slightly below the navel
color	orange
function	procreation, sexuality, physical vitality, creativity
underactive	denial of pleasure, lack of passion, fear of change, frigidity or fear of sex, rigidity
overactive	addictions, emotionally sensitive, obsessive, obsessive-compulsive disorder, overindulgence, jealousy
physical manifestations	uterine and/or bladder problems, lower back pain, bloating, menstrual difficulties, mood swings
gems and crystals	carnelian, orange calcite, dark citrine, coral, gold calcite
sound vibration	vam

Third Chakra: Solar Plexus

location	above the navel, below the chest
color	yellow
function	vitalizes the sympathetic nervous system, digestion, metabolism, personal power, mastery of desire, humor, warmth
underactive	weak willed, easily manipulated, poor discipline, emotionally cold, victim mentality, unreliable
overactive	a need to be right or to have the last word, stubborn, arrogant, overly aggressive, controlling, manipulative, competitive, temper tantrums, violent outbursts
physical manifestation	indigestion, diarrhea, constipation, excessive sugar or salt cravings, middle back pain, excessive thirst, burping
gems and crystal	light citrine, tiger's eye, amber, gold, gold topaz
sound vibration	ram

Fourth Chakra: Heart Chakra

location	center of chest
color	green, pink
function	anchors into the body the life force from higher self, energizes the blood, Divine Love, acceptance, peace, openness, harmony, forgiveness
underactive	critical, judgmental, loneliness, isolation, lack of empathy
overactive	codependency, demanding, jealousy, clingy, overly sacrificing
physical manifestation	chest pain, heart problems, lung congestion, pasty complexion, upper back tension, blood pressure problems, cold sweats, immune deficiency
gems and crystals	green aventurine, rose quartz, emerald, jade, green and pink tourmaline
sound vibration	yam

Fifth Chakra: Throat Chakra

location	throat
color	sky blue
function	creative true gentle expression, speech, kind sharing of wisdom
underactive	fear of speaking, shy, quiet, withdrawn, difficulty articulating
overactive	talks too much, dominating, does not listen, coarse, blunt
physical manifestation	coughing, ear problems, allergies, goiter, stuffy nose, runny nose
gems and crystals	blue agate, azurite, malachite
sound vibration	ham

Sixth Chakra: Third Eye

location	between the eyebrows, and slightly above
color	dark blue
function	vitalizes the lower brain and nervous system, vision, intuition, insight, wisdom
underactive	lack of imagination, easily stressed, poor vision, poor memory, fear, tension
overactive	difficulty concentrating, obsessive, delusions, hallucinations, nightmares

physical manifestation	sinus and/or nose congestion, pain in eyes, headaches, hormonal difficulties, sleep problems
gems and crystals	lapis lazuli, azurite, sapphire, sodalite, lepidolite
sound vibraticn	om

Seventh Chakra: Crown Chakra

location	top of the head
color	violet
function	vitalizes the upper brain, spiritual connection, unifying higher self and personality
underactive	spiritual cynicism, disconnected from source, lack of purpose, fear of death
overactive	confusion, overly intellectual, "trying" to ascend, disconnected from the body
physical manifestation	nervous system dysregulation, poor short-term memory, poor coordination, hallucinations
gems and crystals	clear quartz, amethyst, diamond, selenite
sound vibration	ng

When using a pendulum to assess a chakra, the way in which the pendulum moves indicates the status of that chakra. A chakra can be out of balance in several ways: blocked (no movement of energy), underactive, or overactive. If the chakra is blocked, the pendulum will not move at all. If the chakra is overactive the pendulum will move in an overactive fast fashion. If the chakra is underactive the pendulum will move in an underactive slow fashion. Any amount of blockage, underactivity, or overactivity in a chakra will result in various physical, emotional, and mental difficulties.

When I assess chakras, I will first use the pendulum and then I will ask about various physical, mental, and emotional challenges as a form of cross validation. If the chakra is blocked or out of balance in either direction, that imbalance can be corrected by placing the appropriate crystal on that chakra and directing energy toward the chakra, either with my mind or with another crystal called a terminator crystal. When someone's energy is flowing freely through their chakras and energy field, the person will experience optimal physical, emotional, and mental well-being.

I often start client sessions with chakra clearing and some energy work (especially if the first issue expressed by the client is low energy). Addressing imbalances in the energy body smooths the way for the work that follows. For instance, in a recent client session, after opening the client's blocked root chakra, balancing her underactive solar plexus chakra and throat chakra, she immediately experienced an improved sense of calm and the desire to speak her truth. We then were able to work together on exactly how and when she wanted to put her newfound voice into action.

When I first learned about chakras, I started listening to guided meditations about them. The colors of the chakras would be described during the guided meditations, and I would try to visualize them in myself. Initially, I could not consistently visualize the colors. I found that I had more success visualizing them if I was in a large group of people. The energy that gathers when a large group does a guided meditation together can be very helpful. I believe this is because of the interconnectedness (quantum entanglement) of our energy fields. Over time it has become easier for me to visualize the color of my chakras.

Remember: our energy body extends beyond our physical body.

I have described the seven primary chakras, within the physical body. However, we also have chakras that extend beyond the physical body, above and below. When you do the Central Channel Breath, discussed previously, you are accessing the chakras in your energy field that are above and below the physical body.

Another powerful way of clearing chakras, if you have the opportunity, is to do a sound bath with someone who uses crystal bowls. I do this as often as I can. You can find crystal bowl sound meditations online. My favorite resource for this is Jeralyn Glass at jeralynglass.com.

Optimal Functioning

All these energy clearing and energy healing techniques will enable you to function more optimally—physically, emotionally, and mentally. They can increase your vitality, your compassion, your expression of your true Self, your wisdom, and your clarity. They also will enable you to be more fully alive in your etheric and life force energy, your spirit.

Chapter 10

Working with the Mind and the Mind-Body Connection

The Role of Meditation

*M*y first introduction to meditation was through a Mindfulness Based Stress Reduction (MBSR) course. MBSR is a form of mindfulness meditation that has been rigorously studied and proven to be effective in reducing physical symptoms for patients in medical settings. The course I took was taught by a local practitioner, a colleague in my therapy practice. Mindfulness meditation trains a person to focus on the breath as a way to connect to themselves and be in the moment.

Joining a class was the perfect way for me to get started with meditation and to stick with it. The class met weekly for eight weeks, and there was a basic requirement for the class that I had to commit to meditating every day, throughout the duration of the class for forty straight days! This totally worked for me. Behavioral research has proven that when you start a new habit and do it for a minimum of forty days in a row, it is much more likely that the new behavior will become a long-standing habit. This proved to be completely true in my case.

Many people struggle with the idea of meditating. Meditation is NOT "worshiping a false God." There are many forms of meditation, including but not limited to walking meditation, sitting meditation, and standing meditation. Contemplative prayer, which is taught in the Christian tradition, is also meditation. There are other activities that you may already be doing that have a meditative component to them. For example, sweeping, washing dishes, tying flies, reloading ammunition, certain types of fishing, knitting, and painting are all meditative activities. The key to whether or not the activity is a meditation has to do with what is happening in your mind and where you are placing your focus. While I started with mindfulness meditation, which is not guided and focuses on bringing attention to the breath, I believe guided meditations can also be very helpful, especially for training the brain waves to slow down.

I find great benefit from doing Yoga Nidra, an ancient technique used by yogis in the past (and still used today) for accessing deep states of conscious relaxation. When doing Yoga Nidra, one is guided to relax the body in a very specific way that enables the conscious mind to relax. In this state of deep relaxation the brain waves slow and the body goes into a healing state.

Being able to stay focused in the present moment is a mental discipline. Even after years of doing mindfulness meditation, there are still times—more often than I would like to admit—when I find my mind either replaying a situation that happened in the recent past or creating imaginary scenarios of a future event. At those times I pause, and remind myself how it makes sense that my mind wants to review past events to make sense of them and prepare for the future, especially given the chaotic and unpredictable environment I experienced in my childhood. Once I acknowledge this to myself and practice some self-compassion, I return to focusing on my breath and being in the moment. In that moment, I sidestep the self-judgment.

One of my favorite teachers suggests that when you notice your mind has wandered, silently say to yourself, *Oops*, and return to your breath. What a wonderful way to sidestep self-judgment.

The Role of a Regular Yoga Practice

It is probably no big surprise that my approach to yoga started out from the perspective of the physical. Having grown up as an athlete, initially the idea of doing yoga was not at all appealing. I was the go-go-go kind of person. To me, yoga seemed not interesting enough or exciting enough. If I were to be honest, subconsciously I probably knew that the focus required for yoga would be a challenge for me.

I also believed that yoga was based on some kind of religion and, at the time, I was not open to any teachings other than Christianity. Like many who are raised in the Christian tradition, I was taught to "be careful" about venturing into other teachings.

Yoga is, however, a spiritual path for many. It was years before I considered myself to be a true yogi. Yoga is not a religion, but it does have an underlying philosophy. While I do not claim, at all, to be an expert on the philosophy that underpins yoga, I have become a student of that philosophy over the past fifteen years. How did this happen? I was fortunate. The yoga studios

I joined were studios whose teachers offered philosophy while teaching the poses. Not all yoga studios are like that.

My first yoga studio was an Iyengar Yoga-based studio. The emphasis was on correct alignment. There was a precision to it that was very appealing. At that time, I was not very flexible (physically or mentally). The use of props to allow for appropriate alignment allowed me to accomplish the poses in a way that did not jeopardize my body. There was more emphasis on holding steady in the poses versus flowing quickly from one to the next. This was the challenge and the growth I needed and a wonderful way for me to learn how to truly slow down. I am not exaggerating when I say that, in many ways, yoga changed my life path.

There are many ways in which the practice of yoga can be beneficial. Doing *asana* (the physical postures of yoga) can slow the mind. This is huge if you are someone who is continually attached to and lost in the stories in your mind, which many of us are.

While the idea of doing yoga came across my awareness often, I did not choose to engage in yoga until I was in my early fifties. As I look back, I can see how that was Divine timing. Once I began doing *asana*, over time my mind began to get quieter. From that place of quietness, I became curious about the philosophy and the teachings. I can see now how that transition into curiosity was actually my spirit calling me to a deeper connection with the teachings and the philosophy. My spirit was asking me to go deeper than the physical practice, to discover the richness of the teachings.

Another very important aspect of the deepening of my yoga practice was my exposure to a tantric yogi. Tantric Yoga teaches about being with the struggles of the human experience versus transcending the struggle. Tantric Yoga is about finding within yourself the power to sit with what is difficult and allow your presence to gradually transform the struggle. In Tantric Yoga, life is not seen as a problem to be solved, but rather as something to relish in all its forms.

The practice of being with what feels difficult parallels what we know from psychology and energy medicine to be helpful. Avoidance (conscious or unconscious) contributes to suffering. Being with what feels uncomfortable or difficult breaks the pattern of avoidance.

As a twenty-one-year-old client of mine now wisely says, "The only way past it is through it." She is someone who has struggled for years with patterns of avoidance and is now embracing the sense of power that comes from moving toward things that feel overwhelming (such as working out, applying for school, learning to drive, etc.).

It is so exciting these days to see children, high school youth, and young adults all participating in the practice of yoga, especially given how much the mental body can create roadblocks to a person's connection to spirit and how much yoga helps to slow the mind. It is hard to remember which happened first for me, my mindfulness meditation practice or my yoga practice, but what I know is that the two practices certainly complement each other.

I would like to share a few concepts from yoga that parallel many of the ideas being presented in this book. There are two main ways to look at the philosophy of yoga. The classical teachings of Patanjali as written in the *Yoga Sutras* and Tantric Yoga teachings. Classical yoga philosophy, as taught by Patanjali, is considered to be dualistic—Universal Consciousness is God, and you are separate from God. Tantric philosophy is nondualistic—Universal Consciousness is part of you, and you are part of it.

The Iyengar Yoga-based studio that I joined first followed the classical yoga teaching of Patanjali. Within the teachings of Patanjali, the *Yoga Sutras* state that yoga is the cessation of the movement of thought in the consciousness. (I interpreted "cessation" as stopping or restraining the movement of thoughts). I intuitively knew that there was no way I could cease the fluctuation of my thoughts. It is probably one of the few times in my life when I did not put pressure on myself to accomplish a stated goal.

As humans, we cannot actually stop the movement of thoughts in our consciousness. I adopted a "good enough" approach.

A few years later I was exposed to the nondualistic perspective of Tantric Yoga. This perspective on yoga philosophy taught me that I could choose to make the movement of the fluctuations of thought less active. The emphasis is to slow the flow. The Tantric approach to yoga felt more doable to me. As I practice Tantric Yoga, my focus goes to slowing the flow, by being with what is coming through and consciously directing it to what is more important. As the fluctuation of thoughts is less active, I can more readily experience a peaceful state and see my whole self more clearly. As I practiced slowing the fluctuations of thoughts in my yoga practice, I was simultaneously doing the same in my meditation practice.

There are multiple yoga philosophies. It is important to note that some terms and concepts mean the same across philosophies. For example, *prana* is the term used in yoga for breath and is referred to as your life force. *Pranayama* is the practice of breathing in very specific ways, which ultimately slow the flow of thought, allowing you to become more discerning by putting space between the thoughts. In general, yoga philosophies teach about levels of consciousness and the importance of being aware of what is happening in the activity of the mind. For the purpose of this book, the concepts that follow are from the perspective of nondualism, as in Tantric Yoga.

From the nondual perspective of Tantric Yoga, Universal Consciousness and higher consciousness come through in thoughts, images, and sensations. As you slow the mind and your thoughts, it is in this quiet place that the individual self connects with Universal Consciousness, with Source, with God. The practice of *pranayama* allows you to more fully feel your connection to your spirit. Your spirit, the bigger energy field that is you, is always present. As you slow the flow of thought, by practicing *pranayama*, you can feel your spirit pulsing through you. As you breathe, you are breathing your spirit into your body and can more fully be aware of your connection to your spirit and Universal Consciousness. As you practice *pranayama*, any mental, emotional, or energetic blocks can also be cleared out. This is how *pranayama* clears the pathway for your connection to your spirit and to Universal Consciousness, through awareness.

In Tantric Yoga teachings, *shiva* is the masculine divine and consciousness itself in its most pure and still expression, the unwavering aspect. *Shakti* is the feminine divine or the dynamic flow, power, and energy of consciousness. *Shakti* is the expression of *shiva*. *Shiva* and *shakti* are two sides of the same coin. You are both *shakti* and *shiva*. Another way of thinking of this is to think of *shiva* as the sun (the source) and *shakti* as the sunlight (the energy that emits from the source).

The term *ananda* refers to the bliss and joy you experience as you feel into your connection with the divine masculine and divine feminine and source energy as they flow in the moment. *Purusa* is the term used to refer to one's individual spirit, which is not separate from Universal Consciousness. When we remember that we exist as a blend of divine masculine and divine feminine in reality, that is when we drop into the blissful place of remembering our individual expression of the One. Through the practice of yoga, we have the opportunity to more fully develop our awareness of when we are remembering our connection to Source energy within ourselves, with the ultimate goal of being connected to our strength on the inside while going through the world from a place of softness and empowered awareness. There is emphasis on both the internal and external nature of things.

Sattva is a state of being aware of and in balance with the polarities of life. For example, there is masculine and feminine, effort and surrender, hot and cold, flowing and static, clear and cloudy, hard and soft. *Sattva* is about that sweet spot when we surrender into the awareness of universal support, and move through the world from a place of recognizing our connection to the Divine.

Pratyahara is a practice that refers to embodying our wholeness by bringing our attention to the core of ourselves, our personal source of steadiness and vibrancy. When we do yoga poses (also known as *asana*), *pranayama*, or meditation, we learn to draw into ourselves and connect to our inner resource in order to expand out physically and energetically.

I have mentioned only a few of the teachings of yoga here. The philosophy of yoga is quite complex and comprehensive. To study yoga and its teachings is a lifelong journey. However, you can benefit from yoga even if you never study the philosophy. The practice of *asana* gives you the experience of physical alignment and energy flow. Combined with *prana* and the practice of *pranayama*, you have the opportunity to move into a place of deeper connection with how energy flows in your body and the gift it is to be in a body. The practice of Yoga Nidra, mentioned previously, provides the opportunity to drop into deep levels of relaxation and consciousness and to open to one's spirit.

The practice of yoga has been instrumental in my journey toward a fully embodied experience of life, going through the world with the awareness of how source energy is my copilot. The yoga teacher who has profoundly impacted my life is Tiffany Wood. You can access her and her teachings at tiffanywoodyoga.com.

The Role of Intention-Setting

Having a daily intention-setting practice is a powerful way of continually clearing your mental energy body. Intentions are designed to consciously shift the focus of your thoughts. If you have one or two friends to do this with, it is even more powerful.

When you set an intention, the words you choose are important. You want to state your desired outcome, not what is happening that you do not want or do not like. For example, if I am feeling as though I have closed my heart, I could focus on the intention of "I am opening my heart to myself and others." If I am feeling like a victim of my circumstances, I could focus on the intention of "I am living in joyful abundance and I take responsibility for my life." If I am feeling abandoned or unsupported, I could focus on the intention of "I am living a life supported by my spirit and the Divine Love of Spirit."

If you join or form a supportive group, then all the members of your group can take time every day to think of each other and support each other's intentions. I have experienced that group support by participating in a program called Your Year of Miracles. When we set an intention, the intention has an impact energetically. Vibrationally it takes us to a more open state, more into alignment with our spirit, and to higher and lighter vibrational frequencies.

If you are engaged in an intention practice and you feel resistance, you may want to consider one of the other processes that I am describing, for example, chakra clearing, hypnotherapy, or quantum healing. These will clear out any blockages or resistance.

I want to emphasize the important role of consistency in developing new habits. If you develop a daily habit of bringing your awareness to your energy field and taking steps to clear, rebalance, and re-energize your field, you will experience life more fully from your spirit. Each of us has daily habits, and each of us has the power to choose between daily habits that open us to our spirit or daily habits that keep our energy dispersed and unbalanced. It is a choice. Anytime that you choose a habit or behavior that opens you to your spirit, whether that is an energy technique, qigong, tapping, yoga, breath work, reiki, or meditation, you are choosing to love yourself. If you make that choice from a place of self-love versus duty or responsibility, it will feel better to you.

When considering a choice, you could consider using the intention *I choose me* or *I choose to love myself in this moment* or *I choose to stand in my brilliance*. The energy and vibrational frequency of Love, including self-love is the ultimate healing energy.

Chapter 11

Supportive Trauma Recovery

Recognizing and Understanding Unresolved Trauma

*H*ow do you know if you have unresolved trauma? One key indication is when you have reactions that seem disproportionate to the current situation. We have all had that experience from time to time. After such an experience, you think to yourself, *Why did that bother me so much? Why did I act that way?* You might be aware that you can quite easily feel unsafe, disregarded, ignored, disliked, left out, overlooked, overwhelmed, powerless, or not good enough.

The frequency and intensity of your reactions is an indicator of the amount of unresolved trauma you have. If you find yourself frequently feeling hijacked by your emotions, overtime it can lead to depression and anxiety. Whenever you have a strong reaction to a situation, it is a good idea to ask yourself, *How much of this reaction is really about what's happening right now?*

Your earlier-life experiences always influence your current perceptions and reactions; those experiences create the lens through which you view life and place meaning on events. Overreactions indicate that unresolved emotions are flooding into your current experience. Unconscious beliefs formed very early in life about yourself and the world can be activated by current experiences. The experience can be nonverbal (a smell, a look on someone's face, a turning away). And, if you are using affirmations and it feels as though those affirmations are not holding—or as though they have nowhere to land—supportive trauma processes can be helpful.

How do I know whether early childhood experiences and subsequent subconscious beliefs are driving my own or other people's reactions? A person's past is influencing the present when the following feelings are *often* experienced.

- The need to be in control or to control others.
- The need to please others.
- The need to be the best.
- The need to help others even when you don't really feel like it.
- The need to be the responsible one (and frustration with those who are not).
- The need to be seen as special.
- The need to be left alone.
- The need to get guidance from others versus trusting your own inner knowing.
- The need to be stimulated by endlessly searching for the next exciting thing to do or learn.
- The need to be "tough" or guarded versus open and loving.

- The need to numb yourself with mind-altering substances.
- The need to keep the peace, at great cost to yourself.

In childhood we develop adaptive strategies that enable us to feel safe in our families. If certain feelings were not acceptable to have, we learned to deny those feelings. This led us to denying parts of ourselves. As a child, those strategies were adaptive; they served to help us feel safe and get our basic needs met. However, when those strategies continue into adulthood, they can become maladaptive.

Ways in which our early adaptive strategies can become maladaptive later in life are as follows.

- Pleasing children become adults who do not know their own needs and desires.
- Overly helpful children become adults who do not help themselves.
- Performing children become exhausted workaholics.
- Overly responsible children become controlling adults.
- Overwhelmed solitary children become avoidant loner adults.
- Scared and guarded children become adults who buck the system.

I was a performing and pleasing child. I can remember a pivotal moment, in my late thirties, when a therapist asked me, "What do you need?"

I sat there dumbfounded. As far as I knew I had never been asked that question before. I had never even considered it.

I am now a recovering workaholic who knows what she needs.

Whenever you have what you know is an overreaction—those times when afterwards you think to yourself, *Wow, what was that about?*—stop and ask yourself, *What do I need right now?* And then get busy helping yourself.

We are meant to feel our feelings fully, but not to have our feelings run the show. When you take the stance of observing your emotional reactions, you learn that you are not your feelings, but rather your feelings are simply sensations moving through your energy body and nervous system. When you learn to stay centered, grounded, and connected to your spirit while observing your emotions, then you realize that the emotions have space to come in and go out. When you resist your emotions or ignore them, they have a greater chance of getting stuck in your nervous system and your energy system, ultimately causing maladaptive overreactions.

Try This Exercise: Working Through Strong Emotions

This exercise is intended to be used when you are feeling hijacked by strong emotions.

As always, begin by taking a long slow breath, bringing all of your awareness to your physical body. Now, with eyes closed, take two or three more long deep breaths, and locate the sensation(s) in your body in the moment. As an example, you might have a lump in your throat, a knot in your stomach, or a tightness in your chest.

Bring all your attention to what is happening in your body and let go of the story about what caused the emotion and sensation. Maintain your focus on your body and breathe very slowly, focusing on making your outbreath longer than your inbreath. If you can reach the spot in your body where you are feeling the sensation, put your hand on it, as if to say, "I see you and I am here for you."

Stay with the sensation and allow your breath to move through that sensation. You may notice an image of a smaller or a younger part of yourself emerging. If that happens, notice what that part of you is needing. Try saying aloud one of the following statements to that part of you, whichever seems most relevant.

- You are safe.
- I am here for you.
- You are not alone.
- You matter.

- You are good.
- You are important.
- You are enough.
- I Love you.

This process will offer an opportunity to be present with whatever is happening, while also connecting with your spirit, and allowing your spirit to be present with you. Meanwhile, the wave of emotion comes and goes. Stay with it as sensation versus story and the sensation will shift. Emotion that is held and embraced will melt into love.

You can do this exercise anytime, with any difficult emotion.

After trying this exercise, take a few moments to journal your answers to the following questions:

- How was this experience different from your usual response to emotion?
- What was the original sensation?
- How did the sensation shift after this experience?
- What message, if you offered and then received one, seemed most useful?

Our natural human tendency is to look to other humans for a connection that then translates to the feelings of *I am loved, I am important, I matter, I belong, I am good enough, I am supported, or I am safe.* The problem is that humans are fallible. We are all on a journey and from one moment to the next, we can either be there for each other or be caught up in our own story and our own reactions.

When you reach out to another person for connection, and for whatever reason that person does not respond and the connection does not happen, it feels hurtful. This can happen continually, which sometimes registers as a feeling of rejection on the conscious level, and often registers as rejection on the subconscious level.

It is natural to want the connection from another human, but humans are not consistent. Your higher self and Source are consistently available to you—night and day. When you are focused on people or situations externally, you are giving away your personal power, your sense of power in the world.

Your focus determines your feelings. When you bring your attention back to yourself and connect into your own energy and your spirit, you empower yourself. You are all that you need.

However, this may be hard for you to believe if you had early life experiences where you were abandoned, disregarded, overlooked, abused, put down, or humiliated. As a child you needed the adults in your life to care for you, and you needed to feel accepted by peers. However, once we are grown, if we are still looking for others to care for us or to somehow make us feel good enough, we are operating from our child self.

Only when you transcend the human conditioning can you fully step into your current self, feel the support of your higher self, and Stand in Your Brilliance. One interesting research finding is that people who experience both high amounts of trauma and substantial support are the most resilient.

On a spiritual level, we are meant to be loving, compassionate, generous, empathetic, and respectful. But, the human experience can create wounding, disconnecting us from the greater knowing of our brilliance and the fact that we are here to share love, generosity, and compassion. When we heal the overlay of the human experience, and connect with our higher self, we are more able to bring Divine Love to the world.

Three Effective Trauma Therapy Approaches

In my clinical practice I have specialized in providing trauma recovery therapy to individuals for over thirty years. The three types of trauma therapy that I have seen to be effective and have provided over the years are Eye Movement Desensitization Reprocessing (EMDR), Lifespan Integration (LI), and Complex

Integration of Multiple Brain Systems (CIMBS). Of the three, EMDR was developed the earliest and has the most research to support its effectiveness. Lifespan Integration was developed by an EMDR-trained therapist.

While I discuss these therapies below, detailed information regarding methodology and supporting research, can be found on the following websites:

- emdria.org,
- lifespanintegration.com, and
- complexintegrationmbs.com.

I recommend and endorse these three therapies for many reasons. While each is different in how it is administered, all three involve an inner listening and an allowing of intuition to guide the healing process. I see this process as providing space for connecting with a person's spirit, and allowing Source to support the healing. All three therapies involve focusing on physical sensations in the body, and using awareness to notice subtle shifts in sensation, thoughts, and emotions.

As the person does these things, there is an opportunity to release information (either as an image, an emotion, or a physical sensation) that is stored in the nervous system and throughout the physical energy body. All three therapies enable a person to let go of faulty beliefs in the mental energy body and connect with true beliefs about themself. All three therapies are experiential and depend on an attuned connection with a therapist who holds a calm state in his or her nervous system. This attuned connection between the client and the therapist builds neural connections in the client's brain, which strengthens their capacity for emotional regulation and the ability to access a calm emotional state while observing fluctuations of emotions. Through the therapeutic experience, the client can access and release unconscious beliefs and emotions, and come to new thoughts, new emotions, new physical sensations, and new awarenesses. Their nervous system experiences a release and learns that it is safe to feel the full range of emotions, rather than going through life trying to avoid their inner emotional world.

Because of the nature of the therapies, there is also space for beliefs and emotions from the subconscious mind to arise and be cleared. The outcome of the therapy is that a person can connect with their internal resources and come to realize they have the resources within to navigate the stormy sea of emotions that can happen from time to time. They will then have the freedom to be able to recall difficult experiences in their life without feeling overwhelming tension or distress. The person's system updates to current time, enabling the felt sense that the trauma is over, which puts it in the past for good. From that place, the person is then able to tell the story without reactivating their system. When this happens, there is a deep sense of peace, completeness, wholeness, and safety.

You come to know that your sense of safety lies with your connection to your spirit and that YOU really are all that you need. Once this inner peace and wholeness is realized, any interpersonal connections you make come from a place of security versus insecurity.

Coaching and/or Mentorship

The field of life coaching has expanded greatly over the past ten or so years. Life coaches have a wide range of skills and experience. Some have formal training in counseling and others do not. Many spiritual teachers and some energy healers have certification programs, teacher training programs, or coaching programs.

The coaching and/or mentorship program that I offer is a hybrid program that pulls from all the varying areas of my training. It is highly individualized and focuses on your personal goals for spiritual growth. My mentorship program is a combination of counseling, spiritual support, and life coaching. The goal of the coaching-cum-mentorship that I offer is to support you in healing and living a spirit-guided life.

Because of my training as a mental health counselor licensed in the states of Idaho and Washington, I also pay close attention to times when perhaps a more intensive mental health treatment or trauma therapy would be beneficial.

The Importance of Finding Spiritual Teachers and Helpers Who Resonate with You

There are many amazing spiritual teachers, but they are not all meant for you. It is critical that you pay attention to how you feel when you read or listen to a teacher, or a helper. If the core message being offered by the teacher evokes feelings of shame or not enoughness, that person is not teaching from their spirit.

Inspired help is uplifting, encouraging, and loving. You are meant to look at your shadows and see ways where you may have gotten off track, but your spirit does this in a loving way. Very well-intentioned intuitives, coaches, and teachers can get off track and start guiding from their ego or personality, instead of from Source. After all, they are still human.

Use your feelings as your guide. If the guidance and messages make you feel worse, that is not inspired guidance, plain and simple. There is a difference between the uncomfortable feeling that comes from hearing a message that shines a light on something you have been avoiding and the uncomfortable feeling that comes from a judgmental or shaming message. For example, in my very first session with Sonia Choquette, she said to me, "You think that it is all up to you … [but] you have to be willing to allow yourself to be supported." The funny thing is, in that moment, my first impulse was to leave. She was spot on! It was a hard message to hear, and it also resonated with me. It was exactly what Spirit wanted me to know.

Pay very close attention to whether the message of the teaching resonates with you. If the teacher seems overly focused on wanting or needing a following, rather than being of service, that can be a warning sign. Let your spirit be your guide. Sometimes an uncomfortable feeling may be your spirit giving you a gentle redirection. It is always a good idea to check in with yourself and your inner guidance. Your inner wisdom is your higher self, your spirit. You will know what is best for you by how it feels.

Every day I say a prayer of gratitude for the many helpers who have shown up in my life. Helpers come in many forms. Some of the obvious ones are close friends, family members, special teachers who seem to genuinely care, and possibly coaches. Some helpers may not seem like helpers, in the moment.

The people who have presented the most challenge to you in your life are often present to be your teachers. A teacher is also a helper. These life teachers are present to help you access another part of yourself. To help you grow.

Every experience holds a lesson and an opportunity for growth. Difficulties are sometimes meant to take you deeper.

Some of my greatest, albeit painful, lessons have been as a parent, a sibling, a daughter, and a spouse. I have benefited from supportive family members, loving friends, amazing spiritual teachers, intuitive healers, alternative medicine practitioners, hypnotherapists, psychotherapists, quantum consciousness facilitators, and online spiritual communities.

The more open you are, the more healing can happen. So, why do all of that? Why not just have the human experience? That is fine too. You get to choose. After all, the basis of life is freedom. You get to choose the journey you want to have. And whatever choice you make, it will not be wrong.

On the spiritual level, the soul level, nothing is bad. If you choose not to open to your spirit, then that will be your journey and it will still be in your highest good. But, because you are reading this book, maybe there is some part of you that is curious. Maybe some part of you is longing for something different, maybe even something better. Maybe there is a part of you longing to find your way back home to your spirit. Wherever you are on your human journey, whatever you choose for your healing and growth will be exactly what is right for you right now.

We have the freedom to choose how we respond to our wounding and to our life experiences.

I choose healing. It is my personal choice. I choose alignment. I choose opening to the flow of Spirit. I choose the higher vibrational frequency of joy. I make these choices because, as I heal, I transcend my human conditioning in a way that allows me to bring the full version of myself to the world.

As you heal yourself and bring the full version of yourself to the world, you profoundly impact those around you; and because we are all energetically connected, any healing you do energetically helps others. Healing yourself can help heal the world. The ultimate way to impact the world is to grow yourself and then share that growth.

Remember: We are meant to know who we are in truth, to remember the big-T Truth that we are important, perfect, lovable, worthy of love, good enough, special, powerful, never alone, and pure light, pure spirit. We are also meant to reflect that out into the world so others will remember their big-T Truth . We are meant to stand in our brilliance. We all deserve to feel good and know ourselves in truth.

Letting go of what makes you feel bad is the starting place. Key elements of the process are healing any negative experiences in your life in a way that allows you to release and clear all blockages energetically, emotionally, mentally, and spiritually, and trusting that you are always supported by your spirit and by Spirit.

Chapter 12

Finding Your Way Back Home to Your Brilliance

*Y*our brilliant spirit is your "home." When you come "home" to your spirit, you Stand in Your Brilliance. When you find your way back "home" to your brilliance, then you are open and connected to All That Is. We have different ways of conceptualizing All That Is, including the following: God, the Unified Field, Spirit, Divine Mother and Father, Source, or the Cosmos.

Remember: There's another force at work. Once you are open, aligned, and connected with your spirit, you are back in the field of Oneness from which we all emerge, the field of the nonphysical. You are home.

You will find peace, safety, and security in connecting to your spirit and All That Is. It is a beautiful place of nonjudgment and acceptance.

How Do You Connect to Your Spirit?

The first thing to realize is that you are connected to your spirit at all times, even when you do not know it. Your spirit runs through you and extends beyond you into the nonphysical realms. You are most open to your spirit whenever you are feeling freedom, clarity, peace, expansiveness, appreciation, joy or love. In those states of being and feeling, if you pause to connect with your spirit, as if spirit were another person in the room, you will begin to feel your spirit's presence.

Think of the times when you are most likely to feel joy, freedom, empowerment, appreciation, or love. Where and when does that happen for you? This is very individual. For some, it is when quietly meditating or doing Yoga Nidra. But that is not true for many. Even seasoned meditators will tell you that every meditation session is different and some are not at all joyful or expansive.

In addition to when you meditate, you might already be open and connected with your spirit during the following or other times.

- When on a peaceful walk.
- When sitting or lying on a blanket under a tree.
- When soaking in the beauty of a sunset or a cloud formation.
- When quietly fly fishing.
- When gardening.
- When sewing.
- When dancing.
- When sitting quietly and watching the ocean, the lake, or the river.

- When mesmerized by the flames of a camp fire or a candle.
- When swinging on a swing.
- When playing with or petting an animal or pet.
- When rescuing an animal.
- When participating in a volunteer project (i.e., creek cleanup).
- When doing art.
- When singing or making music.

Whatever it is that brings you joy; that activity will enable you to feel your connection to your spirit. When you are in a place of curiosity, openness, wonder, and awe, you will naturally be more open and connected to your spirit.

Try This Exercise: Activating Openness to Connect with Your Spirit

As always, begin by taking a long slow breath, bringing all of your awareness to your physical body. Then, think of an activity or something that takes you to a state of openness. For example, while gazing at the ocean. Activate that memory, with as much detail as possible. Recall the smells and sounds that occur with that experience. Allow the feeling of openness to build and grow until you have a tangible feeling in your body. You may sense this opening as a lightness, a release of muscle tension, or some kind of feeling of relaxation. Now, flow those sensations of opening through the body using your breath. As you take long slow breaths, allow the sensations of openness to expand even more.

Now, either out loud or in your mind, ask your spirit, "What do you want me to know right now? What is the next important step for me to take?" You could even ask your spirit, "What would you do?" Listen for an answer. When the answer comes, sit with it and ponder it. Really feel into the message and what it might mean if you were to follow it. Trust your inner wisdom. If you cannot hear or sense an answer or a direction, that does not mean that you are not supported or that your spirit is not with you. No answer may be your spirit's way of saying, "Carry on. You are on the right path. You are going in the right direction."

Also, try this exercise the next time you notice yourself already in an open and relaxed state. The more open and expansive you are, the easier it is to feel your spirit. After you have completed the exercise, take a few moments to journal your answers to the following questions.

- What was your spirit's message?
- How did it feel to listen, not knowing if you would get an answer?
- How do you feel now, based on the outcome of the exercise?
- Do you feel worthy of the support?
- Did you experience any cognitive interference? (For example, being distracted in your mind or your mind saying, "This is not going to work for me," or saying something else that creates doubt.)

Going Inward As a Way to Connect to Your Spirit

Going inward is the practice of learning to be in the present moment. It involves being still and bringing your attention to yourself, to your breath, and to the sensations in your body. It is about quieting and focusing. It involves an element of curiosity, and asking yourself, "What's going on in there?"

This is similar to opening a closet or drawer for the first time with the feeling of *I wonder what is in here.*

When you first turn inward and go inside yourself, you may not like what you find. You may find thoughts that are not very nice and images of events in your life that you do not like remembering. It might be like opening a refrigerator drawer to find rotten food. You may already know that there is "stuff" inside that you would rather not see. But, going inward is one of the main gateways to your spirit and to your inner resources. This is because, among the "stuff" inside of you are pearls of wisdom—gems that lead you back to the big-T Truth.

Indeed, among the uncomfortable yucky memories are the memories of times when you felt loved, seen, capable, important, and good enough—if even for a brief time—according to someone somewhere. It may be that the positive resource inside you is memories of when you were offering love, care, or value to another.

You have inner resources—memories of positive experiences; memories of times when you felt loved or protected; your imagination and sense of humor; memories of times when you showed compassion for others; an inner sense of resolve or determination. When you connect with one or more of these resources, it becomes easier to feel your spirit. Then, believing the big-T Truth of who you are becomes easier.

When you focus your attention on the truth of who you are as light and love, you can consciously open up your aura (the energy field that surrounds your physical body) and allow more of the light and energy from your spirit to pour into your beingness.

You may wonder whether you must go inward and quiet your mind to connect to your spirit. Not necessarily. It works differently for everyone; and it will work differently for you from one time to the next.

For the longest time, it was easiest for me to feel my connection to my spirit while walking. I did not even try to do it consciously (FYI, *trying* never works). I would just be walking along in a state of relaxation and ease, and suddenly I would receive a message or get an inspiration. For me, the messages came either as hearing (as clairaudience) or as knowing (as claircognizance). I believe that sometimes these messages are coming from my higher self and other times from guides.

In the beginning, messages and inspiration came to me much more frequently while I was walking rather than when I was meditating. Currently, information and inspiration come more easily while I am meditating. Now, I receive information in the form of images or knowings (intuitive knowledge). Very recently I have learned that when I sense a tension between my shoulder blades, that is my spirit cueing me to open and receive its energy and inspiration.

The important thing is to not put expectations on the process.

Over the years I have worked with a variety of intuitives and mediums. Each of those individuals has had a particular way of teaching me how to receive information. I would try their various approaches, sometimes with success and other times without success. In the end, what turned out to be most effective for me was to practice being open, curious, and trusting.

One of my spiritual teachers once told me to think of it as a game: "Your spirit and Source can be playful too."

If you stay fully present in the moment, in a state of mindful awareness, you will notice times when you get a thought and at the same time you wonder where that thought came from. *Why did I think that just then?* You might even have feelings of excitement as you consider the thought.

The moments you are in a state of ease, openness, and relaxation are when it is easiest for messages from your spirit to get through to you. Your spirit is always present and wanting to connect with you, wanting to guide you, wanting to support you, wanting you to know how much you are loved.

Here is another simple yet powerful example. How many times have you been leaving your home when suddenly you have a thought that you forgot something?

Just the other day I was preparing to go an hour away, to spend the weekend in solitude and write. I had packed my car, including my bag with my computer. I was sure I had packed everything I would need. As I was getting into my car, I had the thought to check and make sure I had the computer's power cord. I heard the thought, but I was sure the computer cord was in the bag. So, I proceeded to get in the driver's seat to leave.

Then, I heard the same thought again.

This time I stopped and looked in my bag, which was in the backseat. Sure enough, the computer cord was *not* in my bag. I had left it at my office.

I thanked my spirit and guides for letting me know and headed to the office to get the power cord. I was so relieved that

I did not drive an hour away, only to discover that I would have to go back to my office.

Your spirit can connect with you in many ways; overtime you will come to recognize the distinct physical signal (a signature, so to speak) that your spirit is connecting with you. In addition to the sensation between my shoulder blades that I mentioned previously, my spirit has a signature it uses to affirm something that I have thought or said. The "signature" it uses is a tingling sensation that starts in my feet and comes up my legs. When I get that sensation I pause to notice what I just said or what I was just thinking. That sensation tells me that my spirit agrees with that thought. It is like my spirit is saying, "YES!"

Other times your spirit and guides and Source will speak to you with signs, songs, or the words of others. Pay attention to animals that cross your path and look up the spiritual meaning for that animal. There may be a message in that for you. Pay attention to songs on the radio that seem to have a message speaking to the moment. Your spirit may speak to you through a passage in a book, or a scene in a movie, or something that someone close by says that really gets your attention.

Your spirit will use things in the physical realm to connect with you and let you know you are not alone on this human journey. Your loved ones who have transitioned back to the nonphysical realm can do this as well. As you get better at noticing the signs, it is important to ask your spirit, "Was that a message for me?" Then ask yourself, "Does that FEEL true?"

I have this unconscious habit of getting overly focused on what *I* need to do; in doing that, I forget the most important truth—that I do not have to do it all by myself. It is not up to just me! I am not in this alone!

Try This Exercise: Opening to Guidance

Once again, begin by taking a long slow breath, bringing all of your awareness to your physical body. Then take a moment to journal your answers to the following questions.

- Are you open to being moved; to being guided?
- Have there been times when you paused to hear and/or feel some guidance? If you have, what happened?
- In what areas of your life are you ready to let go of thinking it is all up to you?

When you open to your spirit, you are opening to the Creator and Unitive Consciousness. When you open and receive, you come to know on a very deep level that you are never alone. You are always supported, guided, and loved. So, wherever you are on your spiritual journey, if you have not yet felt the presence of your spirit or have just recently felt it, know that your spirit has been and is always with you. Trust that your powerful and loving spirit is always there for you; and know that when you clear away the mental, emotional, and energetic blocks, connecting to your spirit will become easier and more natural. Your spirit is always calling you toward well-being. It is the remembering of these truths that brings you back into alignment and Oneness with your spirit and All That Is.

The Power of Imagination

We use our minds to interpret events in our lives and to make meaning of experiences. Our interpretations come in the form of thoughts. Our thoughts influence how we feel. Through the use of imagination, our thoughts have the power to connect us to the feeling states of joy, appreciation, empowerment, freedom, and love.

If you are someone who does not have any positive memories or experiences to access as an inner resource, do not be discouraged; your imagination is your resource and your gateway to your spirit. All you need is the willingness to trust your higher self and the universe, the desire to feel better, and the desire to know and feel your spirit.

When you are feeling joy, appreciation, freedom, and love (either by remembering, imagining, or actually experiencing one of these feelings in the moment), you ARE connected to your spirit.

Here is an example from my life that illustrates the importance of imagination. In the morning, before I start meeting with clients, I often go for a one mile walk along a nature trail close to my office. One morning not long ago while I was walking, I started thinking about the fact that I am still working, and how it feels to still be working when friends and family close to me are retiring. As I thought about that, I started to feel a heaviness, a sort of burdened feeling.

When I noticed that feeling, I decided to turn it around by using my imagination. I asked myself, "What would this walk feel like right now if I was retired?" I used my imagination to pretend I was already retired and out for a morning walk. Within a minute, my feelings shifted to a higher vibrational frequency and feelings of lightness, ease, and freedom. When that happened, I asked my spirit, "What do you want me to know?"

The answer was *You do not have to be retired to feel at ease; the feeling is as close as this.* Consciously choosing to stay focused on this new vibrational frequency of choice and ease intensified and expanded the feeling.

As you go through your days, try to notice the times when you feel more ease and openness. In those moments, have a conversation with your spirit. These conversations pave the pathway for feeling the presence of your spirit. Even if you do not necessarily feel your spirit present, talk to it and your guides, as though they are there. After all, imagine if you were always present for someone—just waiting to help or connect— but the person never asked you for help. Do your spirit a favor and ask for help or guidance. Your spirit is just waiting to connect and to support you. When you are trying to make a decision, put your hand on your heart and ask your spirit for the answer to your dilemma. The more powerfully you ask, the more powerfully you receive.

Following are two exercises that engage the imagination. I learned these techniques from Sonia Choquette.

Try This Exercise: Imagining Beyond Your Fears

As always, begin by taking a long slow breath, bringing all of your awareness to your physical body. Then put your hand on your heart and finish this statement, "If I were not afraid, I would _____."

Be sure to not filter! Go with the first answer or idea that pops into your mind. Write down your answer. Do it again with the same statement, and write down the next answer. Keep going for as long as it feels fun. As you do this over and over (say fifteen to twenty times), your mind will loosen up, you will naturally start filtering less, and your true heart's desires will emerge.

If you have difficulty with this exercise, it may be because you are afraid of the answers. If that is the case, remind yourself that you do not have to actually engage in the answers that come. This is an exploration of desires that are resting just under the surface. Fear resides in the mind. When you set your fear aside, your spirit can help you to see, hear, or just know what you are meant to be doing in your life, both for your good and that of humanity.

Now take a few moments to journal your answers to these questions.

- Were you surprised by what came up?
- Did you filter your answers?
- Did you hold back in any way?
- What sensations did you notice as you did the exercise?
- Would you consider talking to a close friend about your experience with this exercise?

By the way, I never once did this exercise and received the answer that I would write a book. That one must have been buried pretty deep. That makes me giggle.

Try This Exercise: Using Your Body to Sense Guidance

Your spirit can speak to you through your body.

As always, begin by taking a long slow breath, bringing all of your awareness to your physical body.

To learn your "NO," start by saying several statements out loud that you know are not true and see how that feels in your body. Whatever sensation occurs in your body is the sensation that corresponds to your "NO." Then say several statements that you know are true and see how that feels in your body. Whatever sensation occurs with your "YES" statements corresponds to your "YES."

Use simple statements. Here are some examples. For my "NO," I might say, "I am six feet tall." "I have six children." or "I live in Spain." For my "YES," I might say, "I am a counselor." "I have one dog." "I have three siblings."

Alternatively, say the word *yes*, over and over, until you can discern a specific sensation in your body. That sensation is your "YES." Then do the same process with the word *no* until you can discern a specific sensation in the body. That is your "NO." Memorize the feeling in your body. The more you practice this technique the clearer it will become over time. Then, you can get busy going through life following your yeses and steering clear of your noes.

After completing this activity, take a few moments to journal your answers to the following questions.

- What sensation corresponded to your YES?
- What sensation corresponded to your NO?
- How quickly were you able to discern these body sensations?

As always, let it be fun.

**Remember: When you are making choices,
you want to make them from your spirit
and your heart.**

When you combine these techniques for enlisting the inner resource of your imagination with the techniques for clearing blockages in your energy bodies, and have a regular practice of using the breath to come back to yourself, you will be able to more readily make choices from your spirit and your decision-making will be more efficient. Rather than just considering or debating pros and cons (which is deciding from the level of your mind), trust your spirit and let your spirit help you. Use your body, your feelings, and your imagination together as powerful tools to guide you.

All these techniques free you up to make aligned decisions from the place of your spirit. It is quite literally your human self and your spirit making the decisions and choices together. This is living a spirit-guided life. Living from your spirit enables you to respond to life in more creative ways.

Most spiritual teachers talk about pivotal moments in their lives when they chose paths that made no logical sense, but that led them toward fulfilling their purposes in life. Sometimes the spirit-guided choice will not make logical sense. In fact, it may look like a terrible idea from a logical standpoint. But, if your heart and your spirit are calling you in a particular direction, you may almost feel as though you cannot *not* do it. It is in those moments that you will feel the call to trust your spirit and Source.

There Is No Separation

There is no separation between you and your spirit. There is no separation between your spirit and the Oneness of Universal Consciousness. This means that there is no separation between your spirit and the spirits of others. We have our own individual light AND we are all connected. Your spirit is connected to the spirits of your friends, family, and colleagues, as well as what seem like random strangers and acquaintances.

This means that anytime you judge others, you are also rejecting part of yourself.

In addition to that, when you fall into the low vibrational frequencies of pessimism, irritation, impatience, overwhelm, disappointment, doubt, worry, blame, discouragement, anger, revenge, hatred, jealousy, insecurity, guilt, unworthiness, fear, grief, shame, despair, or powerlessness, you are closed down and as a result you are out of resonance with your spirit, with your magnificence, and with the energy and high vibrational frequency of Universal Love. What we think of as "good" and "bad" emotions are high and low vibrational frequencies. Negative emotions (low vibrational frequencies) are your signal to change course and be more open to your spirit, which is always present and flowing through you. Whatever you are thinking when you have those feelings, your spirit does NOT agree with you.

Remember: Your spirit has been with you since the very first moment of your existence and knows everything about you; your spirit knows everything you have ever done; your spirit knows

everything you have ever said and your spirit adores you, loves you, cherishes you, appreciates you and truly understands you. Your spirit knows those times when you have been proud and those times when you have felt ashamed, and your spirit loves you; your spirit knows all of the choices you have ever made and loves you. Your spirit can see the spirit of others and loves them too.

When you are struggling in a human relationship, try to imagine the spirit of that individual. If that person is being hurtful toward you, remember and know that they are out of alignment with their spirit. You can also connect with their spirit and ask their spirit to help. The concept of us versus them is a human concept. On the spiritual level, we are all one; we are all connected.

You are spirit and, by extension, you are God essence in human form. Your God essence is channeled through and to you from your higher self and your soul. This is not a heretical or sacrilegious idea. The energy of Spirit is what breathes you. That is why the breath is so sacred and why we go inward to connect to the breath. God (the Divine Creator) breathed life into All That Is, including the first humans, and you are an extension of that. The energy of the universe is your heritage.

As you open to this knowing, the energy of the cosmos and God can more fully flow through you. It is from this place of fullness that you become your full God essence in human form. This is a choice—the choice to consent to be moved; the choice to consent to be filled up, to receive, to be nurtured, and to be inspired.

But we do not always choose the fullness. Sometimes our will can interfere. Some believe they are meant to suffer. It may be your soul's intention to experience suffering, for the purpose of soul growth. However, it is also possible that you have suffered long enough and it is okay for you to now choose freedom, expansion, joy, abundance, and the peace of being connected to your spirit and the energy of the universe—to feel fully supported and loved. Know that all you want is already available to you.

When you choose freedom, expansion, and joy, you open to receive the abundance that is already here.

I wrote this book so you will know two very important truths. First, you are perfect, beautiful, completely lovable, capable, powerful, magnificent, and good enough. Not because of how you look, who your friends are, or what you are accomplishing. Not even because of how much you help others, but because of your true Self. You are valuable just for being, and you are meant to Stand in Your Brilliance and to shine your light into the world.

Second, you are never alone. When you connect with your spirit and live a spirit-guided life, you come to know this truth on an experiential level.

My passion is for everyone to know these two important truths. Every human being deserves to know these truths, to feel these truths, and to have a spirit-guided life.

Passion Has a Purpose

Knowing your passion is important. Your passion can lead you to your purpose. In yoga philosophy that is called your dharma. Once you know your passion, then you cannot not do it.

My spirit guided me to write this book. It has helped me and hopefully it will help you. Just having the courage to follow my passion has changed me.

The natural result of following your passion is growth. Knowing your passion and following your passion can also change the world. No matter what it is, it will change the world because it is an action that is spirit-guided. Our passions are inspired by our spirit, it is the very plan that you put in place for how you would impact the world in your current incarnation.

Do you know your passion?

Once you are open to your spirit, it will become much clearer to you. Embrace your passion. Follow the nudge. It may feel uncomfortable. In fact, it will likely feel uncomfortable. But it will also feel exciting and meaningful. It does not have to be something that seems "big". Whatever it is, if it is spirit-guided, it will be meaningful and important for the world and the evolution of consciousness.

If you think about others who have inspired you and the things they did, realize that the people who did those things were inspired to do so. They followed their spirit and then that inspired you or touched you in some way.

Wherever you focus your attention, you have the opportunity to bring your light and love into the world. You are on a human journey, and even more importantly, you have the opportunity to be on a journey back to your soul, back to your higher self, back to your spirit. You have the opportunity to Stand in Your Brilliance and live a spirit-guided life in which your human personality is in service to your soul. To live a life full of passion and purpose. To be fully human and fully spirit, bringing your passion to the world.

You may be a scientist making important discoveries, a helper of others, a protector of others, an environmentalist, an encourager, an advocate for the marginalized, an advocate for animals, an artist, an advocate for justice, or a young adult still finding your passion. You can live your passion in a variety of occupations. What you do in the world is important and it is also important to know that the most important purpose for you being here, in this human experience, is to be light and love in the world. This is the most profound way in which we impact the world and the greater consciousness.

Being aligned with your spirit will enable you to be the light, to be the love that you are, and to bring that high vibrational frequency to the world. Bringing your light and love into this world is the most sacred of purposes.

When we go inward and open to our spirit, what we become passionate about will naturally serve a higher purpose. When we listen to the nudge from our spirit and make choices from our heart, we can have profound positive impacts on humanity.

Try This Exercise: Responding to the "Nudge" from Your Spirit

Once again, begin by taking a long slow breath, bringing all of your awareness to your physical body. Then look back on some of the pivotal choices you have made in your life and take a moment to journal your answers to the following questions.

- What is one thing that you feel was a nudge from your spirit?
- Did you follow the nudge?
- If so, what changes were required for you to follow the nudge and embrace the choice you made?
- What was the outcome of this choice?
- What is one thing you want to commit to doing in the future, even though it will take courage and an openness to change?

Opening, trusting, and surrendering are required to live a spirit-guided life. When you say YES to the nudge, you will likely feel some fear, some excitement and, at times, some uncertainty. But, know that following the nudge will lead you to something much bigger in your life.

I often say to my clients, "Spirit has the big road map. There is so much that we cannot see from our perspective."

When you follow your spirit, the choices you make will feel important and meaningful, no matter where your spirit takes you.

There Is Always More

Even though I have learned so much and have grown in so many ways, I intuitively know there is more to come. There is always more to learn and experience. This is the nature of the universe and, by extension, it is the nature of who we are as spiritual beings. That statement may be discouraging if you are the type of person who likes to be able to accomplish things and check them off your list. But, please do not be discouraged. For me, every step along this journey has brought me more joy, more understanding, more magical experiences, and more expansion. It can be that way for you as well.

The universe is limitless and so are you. Know that bliss exists in unexpected places. Growth is the natural outcome of being on a spiritual path and rediscovering the truth of who you are. It cannot *not* be.

That being said, I have been guided to say this as well. The personal growth industry (which includes spiritual growth) is a multi-billion-dollar industry. Many people spend years going to workshops and trainings, and working with coaches and teachers. Much of this is fueled by a deep and sometimes unconscious sense of disconnection.

The answer to your inner peace is not outside you. Inner peace rests in the knowing of your wholeness, and in your connection to your higher self and Source.

After years of continuous study of a wide variety of spiritual teachings, writing this book allowed me to pause and more fully integrate all I have learned along the way. As I stopped looking for more, and opened into the awareness of what I already have learned, I have more fully discovered my magnificence and my connection to All That Is.

My suspicion is that may be true for many of you as well. Consider taking a pause. Sit quietly, possibly by a body of water or in nature. Reflect on what you already know. Consider—this may be the perfect time to trust that your higher self and Source can give you all you need. As you do this, you may naturally discover yourself living a spirit-guided life. Allow yourself to be carried on the wings of Spirit.

Your spirit is always calling you toward well-being. If you are the type of person who is often drawn toward helping others, know that living a spirit-guided life will make all your helping even more potent, even more meaningful. Whatever you choose, rest in knowing you are divinely supported, always. Know that you can trust your spirit and that your spirit is just one breath away. Know you are always meant to Stand in Your Brilliance.

Chapter 13

Things to Use Going Forward

Embracing Change

*E*veryone's journey back to their higher self is different—as different as each individual. My journey started with learning how to be more in the present moment. Ernest Holmes, Eckhart Tolle, Tara Barach, Jack Kornfield, Michael Singer, and Richard Rohr were key to my awakening. Their teachings and books were absolutely critical for me, as I was lost in the stories in my mind, and I did not even know I was!

Understanding the importance of being in the now moment and also experiencing inner calm and presence through meditation and yoga comprised my starting place.

Your starting place may be different. However, being in the present moment is necessary for you to get out of the stories of past experiences. Once you have enough distance from the stories in your mind, you will discover the power of being able to choose how you feel. This does not mean you will never again be sideswiped by faulty beliefs and the feelings accompanying them, but you will at least know it is happening. You will also have greater awareness of when you are beating yourself up with self-criticism and you will have the opportunity to start moving away from self-criticism toward self-love.

Openness is important for having the magical life of alignment with your spirit—openness to new and different experiences. That happened for me when I chose to go to that I Can Do It! Conference and to work with some of the most reputable intuitives, mediums, quantum healers, and spiritual teachers in the field. That type of conference was completely out of my comfort zone, and it was the beginning of my exposure to the power of Spirit. The experiences I had at the conference supercharged my spiritual journey and changed the trajectory of my life, opening me up to amazing experiences I never would have had otherwise. Experiencing the energy and vibration of being in the presence of thousands of people focused on connecting with their spirit and experiencing group past life regressions are just two of the key things that happened for me at that event.

The decision to attend that conference took courage, a willingness to use my financial resources in a less-than-responsible way (or so I thought at the time). The decision required me to surrender to the unknown and open to the possibilities.

Your spirit is always with you and is calling you to make choices that will ultimately lead you back home to your whole self. If you are overly focused on the daily tasks at hand, your usual routine, and the drama of the human journey, it can be hard to recognize the subtle nudges, tugs, and impulses from your spirit. You might miss the guidance.

Professionally, things changed when I shifted more toward emotion-focused therapy techniques and mindfulness-based therapies (like acceptance and commitment therapy—ACT). My spirit was literally talking to me through my heart. Other changes along my journey back to my spirit included learning about the Law of Attraction and applying many of those principles in my life; reading about Christian mystics; learning about quantum physics; and doing my own trauma therapy. Each of these steps were points in time when opportunities presented themselves and I chose to listen to my spirit—to follow the nudge to go outside of my comfort zone and be open to a broader perspective. Oftentimes this meant making a financial commitment to my own growth and healing by having the courage to spend more money than I was used to spending on myself.

Somewhere along the way I let go of holding tightly to my fears around money and dove into trusting that I was being led to something important for me to do in my life; I was being led to something that ultimately would also help others. Later on the journey, it became evident to me that this letting go of my fears around "not enough money" was actually the beginning of truly trusting my spirit, my guides, and Spirit.

It is important to understand that your spirit will lead you one step at a time. Most of the time, you will not see the whole path. Rather, you must just take the step right in front of you.

I have two examples to share. The first is when I heard about a year-long professional training in interpersonal neurobiology and the application to doing therapy. This training involved traveling six hours away for a weekend-long class every other month. I had never made that kind of time or financial commitment before, but I had an overwhelming feeling I was meant to do it.

While the class was very beneficial and it expanded my clinical skills, I do not believe those are the main reasons my spirit guided me to take that class. I believe the real reason was because of someone I was meant to meet there. In that class, I met another therapist who would be instrumental in my life for the next four years. She also was exploring the realm of the metaphysical and how to integrate it with the work of traditional psychotherapy. She joined me in getting my hypnotherapy training and my training in doing LBL regressions. Together we kept each other on the path.

. Another example is when a personal friend started talking with me about *Science of Mind*. For me, this book by Ernest Holmes opened up another way to experience and know God.

This friend was also the first person to tell me about the work of Michael Newton. It is because of her that I am an LBL therapist today. She asked me to go with her to do an LBL regression. I agreed, not because I was especially interested in an LBL regression at the time, but because it felt important.

This friend is aware of her intuitive abilities and, in our intake appointment with the LBL therapist, she turned to me and said, "I just heard that you are supposed to do this."

I have to admit that at first the idea of doing so made my stomach sink and I thought, *No way!* This is a great example of how our spirit will speak to us through others. Over time I accepted the direction, I surrendered my will, and allowed myself to be guided.

Today my LBL work is one of the most passionate parts of my work. I had to overcome a lot of fear and I have experienced incredible growth as a result.

Key Principles To Remember

Here are some truths to remember. Allow these truths to guide you on your journey.

- You are spirit and you can trust your spirit.
- You are a spiritual being on a human journey, and the journey is designed to be for your growth.
- You are NOT your story.
- There are no victims.
- Challenges are an invitation for growth.
- What you think of as "negative experiences" exist to serve you.
- The purpose of the journey is joy. When you go to the vibrational frequency of joy you are living from your spirit. You are free.
- Negative messages and negative experiences early in life take you out of vibrational resonance from your natural state of being and out of alignment from your spirit.
- Getting back into resonance and connection with your spirit and into a joy-filled life is a matter of remembering. Remembering your magnificence will take you back into resonance with All That Is.
- Believing in your spirit's view of you opens you up to feeling worthy of support. Believe.
- Connecting to your spirit helps you to connect to your spirit guides and all the divine support available to you.
- Your spirit and spirit guides are always present and waiting to help. All you have to do is ask.

- Your spirit is always calling you toward well-being.

- Each choice you make matters. The best choices are guided choices—choices made from a place of alignment with and connection to your spirit.

- You are most powerful when you are in alignment with, open to, and aware of your connection to your spirit.

- Awareness is critical. If you are not using awareness, you are letting your subconscious beliefs and your ego run your life.

- Stepping out of your routine, pausing to truly listen, and being willing to follow impulses that take you out of your comfort zone can lead you to magical experiences. BE OPEN!

- Everything happens in divine timing.

- If you are struggling with managing your reactions or if your emotions seem to be running the show, you likely have blockages, imbalances, and/or distortions in your physical, emotional, and/or mental energy bodies.

- You are your best resource. You have a multitude of resources within you, including your spirit and your connection to your divine support. Accessing your inner resources will help you to feel less vulnerable and less dependent on others. You are powerful and can have a powerful life. Trust your inner wisdom.

- Uncertainty is an invitation to surrender and accept what is happening in the moment.

- When you are unsure, pause and be quiet. You will either hear some direction or feel some relief. Just pay attention and breathe.

- When you open to your spirit, you will feel and know your passion and purpose for this journey. You are meant to be love and light in the world.
- You are infinitely loved and supported.

"The Journey"

Feeling alone, abused, disregarded, powerless,

Opening to what is within and to All That Is,

Finding my courage, my belief in myself, my deeper knowing of my power and my value.

Hanging on to that for dear life, hanging on,

Seeing the reflection of my true Self in the gaze and words of others.

Choosing to believe it.

Choosing joy, freedom, fun, independence.

Finding my strength.

Believing in myself, loving myself,

Accepting and trusting where my new sense of Self is taking me.

"You Are Whole"

You are complete.

You are light.

You are love.

You are magnificence.

You are creation itself.

You are a creator.

You are nature.

You are breath.

You are the universe.

You are complete.

You are one with All That Is.

You hold the flame of passion and creative energy within you.

You are here to be all of who you are in the world.

You are here to Stand in Your Brilliance.

You are here to change the world.

Quick Reference Guide for the Exercises

Recommended Reading and Viewing

Books

Batie, Howard F. *Healing Body, Mind & Spirit: A Guide to Energy-Based Healing.* Woodbury, MN: Llewellyn, 2003.

Byrd, Cathy. *The Boy Who Knew Too Much: An Astounding True Story of a Young Boy's Past-Life Memories.* Carlsbad, CA: Hay House, 2017.

Dana, Deb. *Anchored: How to Befriend Your Nervous System Using Polyvagal Theory.* Boulder, CO: Sounds True, 2021.

Eden, Donna, with Dondi Dahlin. *The Little Book of Energy Medicine: The Essential Guide to Balancing Your Body's Energies.* New York, NY: Penguin Group, 2012.

Gallo, Fred P., PhD, and Harry Vincenzi, EdD. *Energy Tapping: How to Rapidly Eliminate Anxiety, Depression, Cravings, and More Using Energy Psychology.* Oakland, CA: New Harbinger, 2008.

Hicks, Esther and Jerry Hicks. *Ask and It Is Given: Learning to Manifest Your Desires.* Carlsbad, CA: Hay House, 2004.

Judith, Anodea. *Eastern Body, Western Mind: Psychology and the Chakra System As a Path to the Self*. New York, NY: Celestial Arts, 1996.

Morrin, Diane, MA. *Untying the Karmic Knot: Healing through Past-Life Regression Therapy, Knowledge through Life-Between-Lives Therapy, The Earth's Future through Progressions*. Indianapolis, IN: Dog Ear Publishing, 2010.

Morter, Sue, Dr. *The Energy Codes: The 7-Step System to Awaken Your Spirit, Heal Your Body, and Live Your Best Life*. New York, NY: Atria, 2019.

Newton, Michael, PhD. *Destiny of Souls: New Case Studies of Life Between Lives*. Woodbury, MN: Llewellyn, 2000.

Newton, Michael, PhD. *Journey of Souls: Case Studies of Life Between Lives*. Woodbury, MN: Llewellyn, 1994.

Pagels, Elaine. *The Gnostic Gospels*. New York, NY: Random House, Inc.,1979.

Peng, Robert, with Rafael Nasser. *The Master Key: Qigong Secrets for Vitality, Love, and Wisdom*. Boulder, CO: Sounds True, 2014.

Riso, Don Richard and Russ Hudson. *The Wisdom of the Enneagram: The Complete Guide to Psychological and Spiritual Growth for the Nine Personality Types*. New York, NY: Bantam, 1999.

Shapiro, Francine, PhD. *Getting Past Your Past: Take Control of Your Life with Self-Help Techniques from EMDR Therapy*. New York, NY: Rodale, 2012.

Smith, Peter. *Quantum Consciousness: Journey through Other Realms.* Woodbury, MN: Llewellyn, 2018.

Tolle, Eckhart. *The Power of Now: A Guide to Spiritual Enlightenment.* Vancouver, BC: Namaste Publishing, 1997, and Novato, CA: New World Library, 1999.

Tucker, Jim B., MD. *Return to Life: Extraordinary Cases of Children Who Remember Past Lives.* New York, NY: St. Martin's Press, 2013.

Weiss, Brian L., MD. *Many Lives, Many Masters: The True Story of a Prominent Psychiatrist, His Young Patient, and the Past-Life Therapy that Changed Both Their Lives.* New York, NY: Touchstone, 2012.

van der Kolk, Bessel A., MD. *The Body Keeps the Score: Brain, Mind, and Body in the Healing of Trauma.* New York, NY: Penguin Books, 2014.

Williamson, Marianne. *A Return to Love: Reflections on the Principles of "A Course In Miracles."* New York, NY: HarperCollins, 1992.

Young, Ed. *Seven Blind Mice.* New York, NY: Penguin Books, 1992.

Websites

www.abraham-hicks.com
www.complexintegrationmbs.com
www.drsuemorter.com,
www.drsuemorter.com/energycodesbook/

www.emdria.org
www.enneagraminstitute.com.
www.instituteforquantumconsciousness.com
www.jeralynglass.com
www.lifespanintegration.com
www.nccih.nih.gov/health/qigong-what-you-need-to-know
www.newtoninstitute.org
www.resourceenergetics.com
www.robertpeng.com
www.soniachoquette.net
www.tiffanywoodyoga.com

YouTube

Abraham Hicks
Prune Harris
The Tapping Solution

Permissions

Acknowledgments

I would like to acknowledge and extend my deepest gratitude to the many individuals who have supported me on my path and have been an integral part of my learning and growth.

To my husband, Paul, who has given me the most profound lessons; has been immensely supportive, patient, and trusting throughout the transformations; and has provided lightness and playfulness at just the right moments. Thank you, Babe, for being my "support team" in every way.

To the hundreds of clients I have had the honor of sitting across from over the years. Thank you for trusting me with your healing and teaching me invaluable lessons about the courage it takes to heal and the power of compassionate presence. Thank you also to the PLR, LBL, QCE, and quantum healing clients who have shared their journeys with me, and the many ways your journeys have contributed to my understanding and ability to help others.

I would like to thank the following therapists, spiritual teachers, mentors, colleagues, healers, and coaches who have directly contributed to my healing, have inspired me to shine my light in the world, and continue to hold the knowing of our magnificence: Howard Batie; Sonia Choquette; Kim Forcina; Erika Greenwell; Dr. Konrad Grzeszkowiak; Dr. KO; Gina Lombardo; Diane Morrin; Dr. Sue Morter; The Newton Institute; Barbara Rose; Marci Shimoff; Peter Smith, Robert Coombs, and Natalie McGrath from the Institute for Quantum Consciousness; Dr. Madison Snevily; Judy Ward; Tiffany Wood; Cindy Wuflestad. Special thanks to Angela Morelli Foisy and Dr. Alan Nasypany for the countless ways in which you have inspired and supported my journey.

I would like to thank the following family and dear friends for the many ways in which you have supported and inspired me. My twin brother, for agreeing to take this journey with me and being there from the start, looking out for me, and celebrating my successes with me. My older sister, for being a key role model of faith and parental love in action. My dear friend Shelley McGuire for introducing me to the teachings of Ernest Holmes, encouraging me to be an LBL therapist, spending hours reading the manuscript for this book, and having conversations that provided even more inspiration. My colleague and friend Brandy Poirier for listening to your spirit when it urged you to come talk to me at that training; for being my companion in the early years of becoming an LBL hypnotherapist; and for the hours of inspired conversation, learning together, and fun. My dear friends Alicia Skelly, Carla Jones, Karen Knoff, and Janet Williams for your loving and caring support.

I would like to thank all those involved in the design and development of the book. Cori Dantini for your amazing artwork and the way you truly captured the spirit of the message of this book. Geoff Affleck for your experience, expertise, guidance, patience, and handholding through the publishing process. Nina Shoroplova for your patience, precision editing, and support.

I will be eternally grateful for Esther and Jerry Hicks and the teachings of Abraham Hicks. Following their teachings, embracing the idea that life is meant to be fun, and learning to take full responsibility for my vibration and the events I create have truly changed my life. I am immensely grateful for the teachings of Deepak Chopra and Eckhart Tolle, and how using their meditations has enabled me to be more in the present moment and to connect to the whole of who I am.

I also want to thank the Your Year of Miracles (YOM) program, of which I have been a part for the past two and a half years. I am grateful for all the other spiritual teachers and healers I came to know through that program, and I want to acknowledge my YOM small group (Elaine, Luisa, Tim, Zane, Carmen, and Diane) for your supercharging of my intentions and for all your support and encouragement.

If not for the continued love and support of these people in my life, this book would not have happened. Each of you has been instrumental in the realization of my dream, and for that I am filled with immense gratitude and appreciation.

About the Author

Kathy Kwiatkowski was born and raised in Fort Lauderdale, Florida. From a young age she spent much of her time playing barefooted outdoors with her twin brother and their friends. She could be found climbing the trees in her yard or playing at the city park. As she got older she spent most of her time, after school and during the summer, playing tennis at the local tennis courts (the same courts where Crissy Evert played). At eighteen, she attended Flagler College in St. Augustine, Florida, where she played collegiate tennis for four years and completed a bachelor's degree in Deaf Education and Elementary Education. For six years Kathy taught elementary-age multi-handicapped deaf children in the public school system in Jacksonville, Florida.

She then moved with her husband to attend the University of Idaho in Moscow, Idaho, where she obtained a master's degree in Clinical Psychology, focusing on child and family therapy. Upon completing her MS, Kathy provided counseling and support services to families with special needs children attending preschool at the University of Idaho Special Education Department. She also offered Family Systems trainings at regional health and welfare programs serving special needs children ages zero to five.

In 1989, Kathy and her husband were gifted the privilege of adopting their first child, their son, at birth. Together, they moved to Seattle, Washington, shortly after their son's birth. There Kathy began working in the community mental health care system, serving children with behavioral and emotional disorders and their families. She did this for three years before moving back to the Palouse area of Idaho, settling once again in Moscow. After working in community mental health for another three years, this time primarily serving children with neglect and sexual abuse trauma, Kathy transitioned into full-time private practice.

In 1997, Kathy and her family were miraculously gifted the privilege of adoption for a second time, when they adopted their infant daughter. Kathy often enjoys telling the story of how both of their children were "gifted to us from the universe."

For the past thirty years, Kathy has maintained a successful private practice. In the past ten years, she has expanded her practice to include spirituality, hypnotherapy, energy healing, and quantum healing. She currently offers individual counseling and mentorship exclusively to clients who are open to approaching their healing from a spiritual perspective. She no longer offers couples or family therapy and has limited the scope of her practice to adults only (except in cases where she is asked to work with highly intuitive adolescents).

Kathy is a certified Life Between Lives (LBL®) facilitator with the Michael Newton Institute, an accredited Quantum Consciousness Facilitator with the Institute for Quantum Consciousness, and a certified Lifespan Integration® therapist.

In addition to working with people individually, Kathy enjoys teaching about spiritual transformation and speaking to groups. She is a reiki practitioner and energy medicine practitioner.

In her free time, Kathy continues to enjoy many outdoor activities. She is most in peace and joy and with her spirit when in nature while boating, remote camping, swimming, hiking, walking, bicycling, gardening, skiing, or sitting on her back patio looking at the sky. She also connects with her spirit regularly by going for walks with her Mini Bernedoodle, Elsa; hitting a few tennis balls now and then; and riding on the back of her husband's Harley Davidson motorcycle. Kathy continues to reside in Moscow, Idaho, with her husband of over forty years, and lives by the Abraham Hicks motto: Life is supposed to be fun.

Author Services

Kathy Kwiatkowski offers individual sessions for past life regressions; Life Between Lives regressions; Quantum Consciousness Experiences; quantum journeying; B.E.S.T. Release quantum healing; energy work; and mentorship for clients desiring to live a spirit-guided life.

For those clients who are doing regression work, energy work, quantum healing, or mentorship, Kathy also offers trauma recovery counseling and support when they are needed, using the traditional healing therapies of Lifespan Integration, Eye Movement Desensitization Reprocessing, and Complex Integration of Multiple Brain Systems.

She also offers Lifespan Integration therapy for therapists seeking LI® certification.

Additionally, she is available for private group speaking engagements.

To discuss any or all of these services, contact her at contact@kathykwiatkowski.com or visit her website, www.kathykwiatkowski.com.